Apostle Scantlebury has penned an apos[...] revelations of Zion and its dimensions. [...] ever read, this book is an eye opener. Whe[...] speak in this manner, the best we can do is to take notes and learn.

—*Apostle Ray Tshitake*
Prophetic Tabernacle Church
Pretoria, South Africa

What a great book! Apostle Michael Scantlebury has written a must-read and compelling study called, *The Restoration Of Zion–Pattern For Building.* Here we learn about how the mission of apostolic and prophetic Believers is being clarified! As "DELIVERERS," we must "go up (ascend) to Mount Zion" to rule and continually establish the Kingdom (Obadiah 1:21, Nehemiah 9:27). *The Restoration Of Zion–Pattern For Building* (the Church) requires the crucial construction of character and substance. Read this book – and learn from one of the best.

—*Dr. Kluane Spake Apostle*
Founder of The School of the Apostles
Atlanta Georgia, USA
https://kluane.com

The greatest hindrance to accurate interpretation and application of Scripture is a futuristic view of Scriptures. This futuristic view of Scriptures continues to rob the Believer of experiencing God in His fullness in the here and now. A contentious subject is that of Zion. In this book Apostle Michael Scantlebury draws parallels between Zion as a physical place that existed in history and Zion as a model/pattern of building. He takes us on a journey where he explains in detail the language of the times and its current application. He positions Zion as an ever-present reality of the 21st Century Church. This book will shift us into a working model of Zion and not just a sentimental view of it on which fulfilment of all things prophetically is dependent. When we understand Zion within a 21st Century Church context we will change the way we do Church.

—*Apostle Brandon Bailey*
Senior Elder Teleios Church
Johannesburg, South Africa

Apostle Michael Scantlebury has once again given us another prophetic revelation concerning the restoration of the true nature of the New Testament Church. Apostle Scantlebury reveals that the Church is the resting place for the Presence of the Spirit of the Lord.

As you read this book you will discover the nature of Zion as the Body of Christ, which is built upon the foundation of the Apostles and Prophets, and Jesus Christ the chief cornerstone of Zion. Apostle Scantlebury has a unique ability to compare Scripture with Scripture compelling the leadership of the Body of Christ to reconsider traditional doctrine.

Apostle is giving us prophetic revelation that brings us into Present Truth, also he is urging the leadership of the Church of the Lord Jesus to embrace this revelation of the Kingdom of God, and embrace the restoration of Zion. This book gives us a blueprint and pattern. *The Restoration Of Zion–Pattern For Building*, is a must read for every Apostolic Leader to upgrade the Body of Christ. The Church is the Zion of The Lord Jesus Christ.

—*Apostle Sylvester Trotter*
New Jerusalem Ministries
Mobile Alabama, USA

We recognize that the Church is on the threshold of a global harvest. I have found this book to be truly inspirational in laying out God's pattern for this Kingdom age that we are living in. The book gives us the Believer an accurate understanding of God's prophetic restoration of Zion the spiritual House of God, which in the time we live calls for Believers to rise up in their high calling to fulfil divine destiny and purpose. This book shows us how we can build our Ministries, and churches using revelatory blueprints from the lives of David and various scriptural examples to enjoy the miraculous life Christ had for all of us. A truly enjoyable read!

—*Apostle Chucks Ajuka*
Fresh Fire Ministries
London Road Mitcham
Surrey, England

I am thankful for the ministry of Apostle Michael Scantlebury, who is truly a builder in the Lord's Church.

One of the ways our King releases His authority into the lives of His people is to give us anointed authors, who pen the pathway for those to "see" clearly His ways. Apostle Michael is one such author.

In this resource, *The Restoration Of Zion–Pattern For Building*, Apostle Michael continues releasing the grace to build a people in the earth for God to dwell in called Zion. It is from Zion the glory flows with praise and worship, salvations, miracles and the beauty of the righteousness and holiness of God flowing in the earth.

From looking at Earthly Zion to embracing Heavenly Zion it is a journey from pride and faithlessness to humility, unity and victory. It is a resource of hope.

As a man given to seeing cities transformed by relationship and unity, I was particularly blessed, as Apostle Michael unveils to us a place called 'Hebron.'

I recommend this book to all who are seeking to build and disciple a people, who have ceased from their own works, and yielding to Spirit-led kingdom living. A church the gates of hell shall not prevail against, world without end.

—Daryl O'Neil, Apostle
Ruach Church
Barnabus Apostolic Alliance
Chicago IL, USA

Apostle Michael Scantlebury's new release, *The Restoration Of Zion–Pattern For Building* is a well-prepared masterpiece. He has authored this new release as well as many others. His publications will continue to bless you and renew your faith. Apostle's new book release is full of much wisdom and revelation with biblical accuracy, which assures his teachings are in line with the apostolic doctrine. This read will guarantee growth and maturity within the Body Of Christ! I was completely blessed when I read the part regarding "The Trumpet Is Being Blown In Zion!"

—Apostle Mary D. Lewis,
ASAPTT Network LLC, /School
Waldorf, MD, USA

Michael Scantlebury writes brilliantly about the shift from Old Testament types to New Covenant realities. He succinctly describes the spiritual and practical outworking of God's Old Testament Patterns in this 'Now' Kingdom season. This book, *The Restoration Of Zion–Pattern For Building* emphasises revelatory interpretation of God's eternal blueprints for effective, productive church expression. I believe this book is a timely word from God for all those leading churches and ministries. God's will is done when we build according to His pattern!

—Philip M Spence (Apostle)
Jabez International Mission
Kingdom Life Church
Brisbane, Australia

I believe this book will help the local church and its leadership, equip them into a new dimension of how to build according to the Kingdom blueprint laid out in each chapter. Understanding what Restoration and Zion means, is vital for the fulfilment of God's master plan for His Church. Dr. Scantlebury through the revelation of the Holy Spirit brings to life a missing principle that is desperately needed in the Body of Christ. I believe you will not just be blessed by this book but see with new eyes the revelation of Zion.

—David Tobie VanderWalt, Pastor
Legacy Life Church
Port Elizabeth, South Africa

For any Church leader that has a desire to shift and build... this on time book *The Restoration Of Zion–Pattern For Building*, will give you an 'Aha' moment to come up higher to reset God's original intentional design, as He dwells among us!

—Tyrone McFarland, Pastor,
Legacy Life Church,
Orlando Florida, USA

MICHAEL SCANTLEBURY

THE RESTORATION OF ZION

PATTERN FOR BUILDING

THE RESTORATION OF ZION—PATTERN FOR BUILDING
Copyright © 2019 by Michael Scantlebury

Editorial Consultants:
Anita Thompson – 604-521-6042

Cover design by: Michelle of Ryele Studios – https://ryele.co/

All Scripture quotations, unless otherwise indicated, are taken from the New King James Version. Copyright © 1982 by Thomas Nelson, Inc. Used by permission. All rights reserved. • Scriptures marked (KJV) are taken from the Holy Bible, King James Version, which is in the public domain. • Scriptures marked (NIV) are taken from the Holy Bible, New International Version®, NIV® Copyright ©1973, 1978, 1984, 2011 by Biblica, Inc.® Used by permission. All rights reserved worldwide.

Scripture throughout the text is indicated with italics. Words in roman (regular) text within Scripture quotations have been added by the author for emphasis. Please refer directly to the Biblical translations presented for the original representation.

Hebrew and Greek definitions are from James Strong, Strong's Exhaustive Concordance of the Bible (Peabody, MA: Hendrickson Publishers, n.d.).

Michael Scantlebury has taken author's prerogative in capitalizing certain words that are not usually capitalized according to standard grammatical practice. Also, please note that the name satan and related names are not capitalized as we choose not to acknowledge him, even to the point of disregarding standard grammatical practice.

ISBN: 978-1-4866-1878-1
eBook ISBN: 978-1-4866-1879-8

Word Alive Press
119 De Baets Street Winnipeg, MB R2J 3R9
www.wordalivepress.ca

WORD ALIVE
—P R E S S—

Cataloguing in Publication information is can be obtained from Library and Archives Canada.

BOOKS BY MICHAEL SCANTLEBURY

As It Was In The Beginning
Daniel In Babylon – The Study Guide
Principles For Victorious Living Volume II
Principles For Victorious Living Volume I
Present Truth Lifestyle – Daniel In Babylon
Esther: Present Truth Church
The Fortress Church
Called to be An Apostle – An Autobiography
Leaven Revealed
Five Pillars of The Apostolic
Apostolic Purity
Apostolic Reformation
Jesus Christ The Apostle and High Priest of Our Profession
Kingdom Advancing Prayer Volume I
Kingdom Advancing Prayer Volume II
Kingdom Advancing Prayer Volume III
Internal Reformation
God's Nature Expressed Through His Names
"I Will Build My Church." – Jesus Christ
Identifying and Defeating The Jezebel Spirit

Table Of Contents

FOREWORD

IN THIS BOOK *THE RESTORATION OF ZION–PATTERN FOR BUILDING*, APOSTLE Michael Scantlebury has vividly taken us through the Scriptures to show us clearly the heart's desire of God concerning Zion and more importantly to reveal the exact concept for building Zion in this present season.

King David moved the Ark of the Covenant [the symbol of God's Presence among His people] to the Tabernacle of David in Zion and not to the Tabernacle of Moses in Gibeon. This unusual move had God's approval.

Psalm 132:13-14 says,

For the Lord has chosen Zion; He has desired it for His dwelling place: "This is My resting place forever; Here I will dwell, for I have desired it."

King David by revelation understood the longing of the heart of God, which is Zion as His dwelling place, and he was able to establish this heart desire of God. Thus, it proves to be reasonable why God said of David that he was "**A Man After My Own Heart**".

God was pleased with the Tabernacle of David because everyone could now come before God's Presence in this plain tent in Zion without any veil or restriction, and there, freely worship the LORD. The ultimate vision of Zion is a restoration of something that has been lost to the Church, a free access to God's Presence.

The line of thinking is that if something has "fallen down" that it will be restored or rebuilt. This restoration or rebuilding does not refer to a physical temple in Jerusalem as many end-time eschatological teachers are proclaiming, but it is the restoration of the Church and of God's spiritual Kingdom that is being established so everyone can have full and free access to God's Presence.

But as Apostle Michael Scantlebury has shown, "the building of the temple [*tabernacle*] is the building of His Church. Not by stone, or brick or precious gems, but the building of character and substance in the Believer until Christ be formed".

This building of the Tabernacle is not the reconstruction of the Davidic temple but it needs a designated person(s) to lead this building project for the complete restoration of Zion! And God in His wisdom has appointed Apostles and Prophets as the wise master builders who receive and understand by revelation the building blueprints from Heaven".

Zion is the dwelling place of God where the Ark of the Covenant was placed in the Tabernacle of David.

The prophetic edict of God is about Zion – The Restoration of the Tabernacle of David, through the Body of Believers—The Church.

Amos 9:11 says,

On that day I will raise up The tabernacle of David, which has fallen down, And repair its damages; I will raise up its ruins, And rebuild it as in the days of old;

Acts 15:16 says,

After this I will return And will rebuild the tabernacle of David, which has fallen down; I will rebuild its ruins, And I will set it up;

I highly endorse the teachings of this book and I recommend this to every Believer who is in pursuit of God's eternal purpose to establish His heart's desire – Zion, because the author has done an excellent job to pen down the prophetic plan of God.

Thanks Apostle Michael Scantlebury for revealing to us God's pattern. Keep it coming!

Yours for the sake of God's purpose!

—Apostle Israel Onoriobe
World Vision Crusade Outreach Ministries
Cape Town – South Africa
www.wvcom-international.org

INTRODUCTION

THE WORD ZION OCCURS OVER 150 TIMES IN THE BIBLE. IT ESSENTIALLY MEANS "fortification" and has the idea of being "raised up" as a "monument." Zion is described both as the city of David and the city of God. As the Bible progresses, the word Zion expands in scope and takes on an additional spiritual meaning.

In Amos 9:11 we read the following *"On that day I will raise up The tabernacle of David, which has fallen down, And repair its damages; I will raise up its ruins, And rebuild it as in the days of old;"*

This same promise was made in the New Testament in Acts 15:16-17 *"After this I will return And will rebuild the tabernacle of David, which has fallen down; I will rebuild its ruins, And I will set it up; So that the rest of mankind may seek the LORD, Even all the Gentiles who are called by My name, Says the LORD who does all these things."*

Does this signify the rebuilding of the physical temple of the Old Testament? With the constant turmoil in the Middle East, many Bible believing Christians speculate about whether the Jewish temple will be rebuilt in the months and years to come. Entire Christian ministries have been raised up to help build the temple and to hasten the return of Jesus Christ. For those espousing this view (and they are many), such an event will signal the start of the "last days", the final events of earth's history and of course this depends on your views regarding eschatology.

However, as we study the Word, one of the things that truly resonates is the need to build what the Lord has desired and instructed in terms of a temple and not an opulent building where we expect Him to come and commune with us. Will we go so far as to offer blood sacrifices and find a lineage of High Priests to sacrifice for our sins again, after Jesus came to earth and is our sacrificial Lamb. A rebuilding of a physical third temple for sacrifice today would be as useless as it was then, and it would not be the House of God.

The New Testament documents the idea that the Temple is the Body of Believers in Jesus Christ. In this regard, I submit that one of the charges given to Apostles and Prophets is to build according to the blueprint from Heaven, according to what God wants, as recorded in Ephesians 2:19-22, which says,

> *Now, therefore, you are no longer strangers and foreigners, but fellow citizens with the saints and members of the household of God, having been built on the foundation of the apostles and prophets, Jesus Christ Himself being the chief cornerstone, in whom the whole building, being fitted together, grows into a holy temple in the Lord, in whom you also are being built together for a dwelling place of God in the Spirit.*

Hence, the building of the Temple is the building of His Church. Not with stone, or brick or precious gems, but the building of character and substance in the Believer's life until Christ be formed. And, the responsibility lays on us to be constantly seeking the Lord to hear what He has to say when it comes to the building of His Church, Mount Zion.

CHAPTER ONE
A BRIEF HISTORY ABOUT EARTHLY ZION

WHEN YOU THINK OF ZION, WHAT DOES IT CONJURE UP IN YOUR MIND? WE HEAR about Zionism, and do we fully know what it is? As Christians we have sung the choruses and the hymns about Zion or Mount Zion, but do we fully understand just what we are singing about? The Bible promises the full restoration of Zion, and if we do not understand what Zion is, how and what do we anticipate in terms of its restoration?

The songs we sing from rote and memory hold a much deeper application for the Christian in terms of the City of Zion and the Mountain of Zion, but also, let's explore historically how Zionism got its start.

Zionism in the secular sense is Israel's national ideology. Zionists believe Judaism is a nationality as well as a religion, and that Jews deserve their own state in their ancestral homeland, Israel, in the same way the French people deserve France or the Chinese people should have China. This nationalism is what spearheaded the movement of Jews immigrating to Israel in the first place.

Jews can in reality trace their nationhood back to the biblical kingdoms of David and Solomon, circa 950 BC. But like myself, some of you may have wondered if the "calling" to return to Israel for the Jews born abroad was innate or learned as many Jews have never been to Israel, do not know it as home, have little idea about it, but there is a drive within them that they do everything in their power to get there. There is even an organization that transports Ethiopian Jews to Israel one at a time when funding is procured. (International Fellowship of Christians and Jews)

Modern Zionism has nothing to do with the spiritual promise of the re-establishment of the holy city. Zionism was built on the longstanding Jewish yearning for a "return to Zion" based on Jewish nationalism. It all came about in the 19th Century when a secular Austrian-Jewish journalist, Theodor Herzl, was the first to turn rumblings of Jewish nationalism into an international movement around 1896.

Herzl witnessed brutal European anti-Semitism firsthand, and became convinced the Jewish people could never survive outside of a country of their own. He wrote essays and organized meetings that spurred mass Jewish emigration from Europe to what's now Israel/Palestine. Before Herzl, about 20,000 Jews lived in Israel; by the time Adolf Hitler came to power in Germany, the number was about eight times that. As nationalism rose in Europe, the Jews immigrated in droves to Israel.

Though Zionists all agree that Israel should exist, they've long disagreed on what its government should look like. In the most general terms, the Zionist left, which dominated the country's politics until the late 1970s, is inclined to trade Israeli-controlled land for peace with Arab nations, wants more government intervention in the economy, and prefers a secular government over a religious one. The Zionist right, which currently enjoys commanding positions in the Israeli government and popular opinion, tends to be more skeptical of "land-for-peace" deals, more libertarian on the economy, and more comfortable mixing religion and politics.

Arabs and Palestinians generally oppose Zionism, as the explicitly Jewish character of the Israeli state means that Jews have privileges that others don't. For instance, any Jew anywhere in the world can become an Israeli citizen, a right not extended to any other class of person. Arabs, then, often see Zionism as a species of colonialism and racism aimed at appropriating Palestinian land and systematically dis-enfranchising the Palestinians that remain. Arab states actually pushed through a UN General Assembly resolution labeling Zionism "a form of racism and racial dis-crimination" in 1975, though it was repealed 16 years later." (Partially sourced from Wikipedia)

As Believers in Jesus Christ, we do not have an innate calling to immigrate to Israel, nor is our interest in Zion and its restoration as one of political or national interest. We are not waiting for Messiah as we have Him living within us but the establishment of Zion remains a very important event in the lives of the Believers. We shall see according to the Scriptures where God has a completely different plan concerning Zion. He promises to restore Zion, not in the physical sense of a country or a temple. As a matter what I have come to realize is that earthly Zion no longer holds any significance for the Christian, but the spiritual Zion ... that is another story. However, we need to consider the word "restoration" and how it impacts Zion for the Believers in Jesus Christ before we move on.

CHAPTER TWO
MEANING OF THE WORD RESTORATION

JUST WHAT IS RESTORATION? WHEN SOMETHING IS IN NEED OF RESTORATION, the original structure has been damaged or has become dilapidated. Restoration brings an edifice to life and preserves the original beauty and architecture. To be restored is not a negative thing, as it continues to sustain the edifice in its architectural beauty. The human heart can be restored as well, and as Believers we are waiting for the restoration of Zion as per the many references in Scripture we have read. It speaks to something good occurring.

The word restoration has its root meaning in several Greek and Hebrew words. For example:

In the Greek it is the word Apokatastasis (ap-ok-at-as'-tas-is)—From apo, "back, again," kathistemi, "to set in order," also means: restore back to original standing, i.e. that existed before a fall; *re-establish*, returning back to the (ultimate) ideal; (figuratively) restore back to *full freedom* (the *liberty* of the original standing); to *enjoy again*, i.e. what was taken away by a destructive or life-dominating power. (From the Strong's Concordance)

This meaning in particular is used in Acts 3:21, which states: *whom heaven must receive until the times of restoration of all things, which God has spoken by the mouth of all His holy prophets since the world began.*

Another Greek word for restoration is Katartizo (kat-ar-tid'-zo), which means—"To mend, to furnish completely."

And lastly, in the Hebrew it is the word chadash (khaw-dash'), which means, "To renew, repair."

Since we have now established the meaning of this word according to the Scriptures, let us begin by taking a look at what Zion encompasses and its biblical applications and why the Scriptures, promise a full restoration in the next chapter.

CHAPTER THREE
A LOOK AT ZION AND IT'S APPLICATIONS

THE WORD ZION OCCURS OVER 150 TIMES IN THE BIBLE. IT ESSENTIALLY MEANS "fortification" and has the idea of being "raised up" as a "monument." Zion is described both as the city of David and the city of God. As the Bible progresses, the word Zion expands in scope and takes on an additional spiritual meaning.

Psalm 87:2–3 says,

The LORD loves the gates of Zion More than all the dwellings of Jacob. Glorious things are spoken of you, O city of God!

As we have read here, Zion is synonymous with the city of God, and it is a place that God loves. Zion was also located in Jerusalem. It was also the high hill on which king David built a citadel.

The first mention of Zion in the Bible is found in 2 Samuel 5:7, which says,

Nevertheless David took the stronghold of Zion (that is, the City of David).

Zion was originally an ancient Jebusite fortress in the city of Jerusalem. After David's conquest of the fortress, Jerusalem became a possession of

Israel. The royal palace was built there, and Zion/Jerusalem became the seat of power in Israel's kingdom.

When Solomon built the Temple in Jerusalem (2 Chronicles chapter 3), the meaning of Zion expanded further to include the temple area as seen in the following:

Psalm 2:6 says,

Yet I have set My King On My holy hill of Zion.

Psalm 48:2 says,

Beautiful in elevation, The joy of the whole earth, Is Mount Zion on the sides of the north, The city of the great King.

Psalm 132:13 says,

For the LORD has chosen Zion; He has desired it for His dwelling place:

This is the meaning found in the prophecy of Jeremiah 31:6, which states: *Come; let us go up to Zion, to the LORD our God.*

In the Old Testament Zion is used as a name for the city of Jerusalem: Isaiah 40:9 says,

O Zion, You who bring good tidings, Get up into the high mountain; O Jerusalem, You who bring good tidings, Lift up your voice with strength, Lift it up, be not afraid; Say to the cities of Judah, "Behold your God!"

The land of Judah:
Jeremiah 31:12 says,

Therefore they shall come and sing in the height of Zion, Streaming to the goodness of the LORD—For wheat and new wine and oil, For the young of the flock and the herd; Their souls shall be like a well-watered garden, And they shall sorrow no more at all.

And the nation of Israel as a whole:
Zechariah 9:13 says,

For I have bent Judah, My bow, Fitted the bow with Ephraim, And raised up your sons, O Zion, Against your sons, O Greece, And made you like the sword of a mighty man.

Zion is also used in a theological or spiritual sense in Scripture. In the Old Testament *Zion* refers figuratively to Israel as the people of God as revealed in Isaiah 60:14, which says,

Also the sons of those who afflicted you Shall come bowing to you, And all those who despised you shall fall prostrate at the soles of your feet; And they shall call you The City of the LORD, Zion of the Holy One of Israel.

In the New Testament, Zion refers to God's spiritual Kingdom. We have not come to Mount Sinai, says the Apostle, *But to Mount Zion and to the city of the living God, the heavenly Jerusalem, to an innumerable company of angels.* Hebrews 12:22

Apostle Peter, quoting Isaiah 28:16, refers to Christ as the Cornerstone of Zion: *Therefore it is also contained in the Scripture, "Behold, I lay in Zion A chief cornerstone, elect, precious, And he who believes on Him will by no means be put to shame."* 1 Peter 2:6

Isaiah 52:8 speak about the Restoration of Zion and building according to the proper blueprint. Let's read verses 7-8, which says,

How lovely on the mountains Are the feet of him who brings good news, Who announces peace And brings good news of happiness, Who announces salvation, And says to Zion, "Your God reigns!" Listen! Your watchmen lift up their voices, They shout joyfully together; For they will see with their own eyes When the LORD restores Zion.

To better understand Zion let us go back to when it was first established. Psalm 132:1-18 gives us some very important information about the significance of Mount Zion. In the first few verses what David was saying was that no rest would be found by him, not even in his own house, until the Lord could rest in His holy dwelling place, His House! Here is what it says,

> LORD, remember David And all his afflictions; How he swore to the LORD, And vowed to the Mighty One of Jacob: "Surely I will not go into the chamber of my house, Or go up to the comfort of my bed; I will not give sleep to my eyes Or slumber to my eyelids, Until I find a place for the LORD, A dwelling place for the Mighty One of Jacob." Behold, we heard of it in Ephrathah; We found it in the fields of the woods. Let us go into His tabernacle; Let us worship at His footstool. Arise, O LORD, to Your resting place, You and the ark of Your strength. Let Your priests be clothed with righteousness, And let Your saints shout for joy. For Your servant David's sake, Do not turn away the face of Your Anointed. The LORD has sworn in truth to David; He will not turn from it: "I will set upon your throne the fruit of your body. If your sons will keep My covenant And My testimony which I shall teach them, Their sons also shall sit upon your throne forevermore." For the LORD has chosen Zion; He has desired it for His dwelling place: "This is My resting place forever; Here I will dwell, for I have desired it. I will abundantly bless her provision; I will satisfy her poor with bread. I will also clothe her priests with salvation, And her saints shall shout aloud for joy. There I will make the horn of David grow; I will prepare a lamp for My Anointed. His enemies I will clothe with shame, But upon Himself His crown shall flourish."

Does this signify the rebuilding of the physical temple of the Old Testament? With the constant turmoil in the Middle East, many Bible believing Christians speculate about whether the Jewish temple will be rebuilt in the months and years to come. Entire Christian ministries have been raised up to help build the temple to hasten the return of Jesus Christ. For those espousing this view (and they are many), such an event will signal the start of the "last days", the final events of earth's history and of course this depends on your views regarding eschatology.

Just as many Christians misplace the focus from spiritual Israel to the literal Jewish nation being resettled and rebuilt, they have also confused what the Bible says on the subject of the temple. These Christian Zionists' speculation about the erection of a new temple to replace the old one stems from a vague reference in 2 Thessalonians chapter 2 KJV dealing with the Antichrist power, it states: *That day shall not come ... [until] that man of sin be revealed, the son of perdition; Who opposeth and exalteth himself above all that is called God, or that is worshipped; so that he as God sitteth in the temple of God, shewing himself that he is God* (vs. 3, 4). Their stream of thought is that if Antichrist will sit in the temple, it therefore needs to be rebuilt.

Much has been written on this view of the Scriptures. Popular writers such as Hal Lindsey, Tim LaHaye, and John Hage support this view and their published book sales exceed 70 million copies—including the popular Left Behind series. Their beliefs are endorsed by some of the largest theological colleges and institutions.

However, as we study the Word, one of the things that truly resonates is the need to build what the Lord has desired and instructed in terms of a temple and not an opulent building where we expect Him to come and commune with us. Will we go so far as to offer blood sacrifices and find a lineage of High Priests to sacrifice for our sins again, after Jesus came to earth and is our sacrificial Lamb. A temple for sacrifice today would be as useless as it was then, and it would not be the House of God.

The New Testament documents the idea that the Temple is the Body of Believers in Jesus Christ. In this regard, I submit that one of the charges given to Apostles and Prophets is to build according to the blueprint from Heaven, according to what God wants, as recorded in Ephesians 2:19-22, which states,

> *Now, therefore, you are no longer strangers and foreigners, but fellow citizens with the saints and members of the household of God,* having been built on the foundation of the apostles and prophets, Jesus Christ Himself being the chief cornerstone, *in whom the whole building, being fitted together, grows into a holy temple in the Lord, in whom you also are being built together for a dwelling place of God in the Spirit."*

Hence, the building of the temple is the building of His Church. Not by stone, or brick or precious gems, but the building of character and substance in the Believer until Christ be formed. And, the responsibility lays on us to be constantly seeking the Lord to hear what He has to say when it comes to the building of His Church, Mount Zion.

We will digress to the Old Testament to consider three examples involving men who had been told by God to build something according to heavenly and Godly blueprints. The first man was Noah—God told Noah to build an Ark so that his house could be saved. God gave him instructions and specifications, which were to be followed to the letter. You can read the entire account in Genesis chapters 6-9. Having said that let me cite a few verses from chapter 6 here:

Genesis 6:13-18 says,

And God said to Noah, "The end of all flesh has come before Me, for the earth is filled with violence through them; and behold, I will destroy them with the earth. Make yourself an ark of gopherwood; make rooms in the ark, and cover it inside and outside with pitch. And this is how you shall make it: The length of the ark shall be three hundred cubits, its width fifty cubits, and its height thirty cubits. You shall make a window for the ark, and you shall finish it to a cubit from above; and set the door of the ark in its side. You shall make it with lower, second, and third decks. And behold, I Myself am bringing floodwaters on the earth, to destroy from under heaven all flesh in which is the breath of life; everything that is on the earth shall die. But I will establish My covenant with you; and you shall go into the ark—you, your sons, your wife, and your sons' wives with you."

Moses was the second man given specific instructions for building. He was commissioned to build the first Tabernacle as recorded in the book of Exodus. Here is a brief excerpt to highlight my point:

Exodus 25:1, 8-16 says,

Then the LORD spoke to Moses, saying: "And let them make Me a sanctuary, that I may dwell among them. According to all that I show you, that is, the pattern of the tabernacle and the pattern of all its furnishings, just so you shall make it. And they shall make an ark of acacia wood; two and a half cubits shall be its length, a cubit and a half its width, and a cubit and a half its height. And you shall overlay it with pure gold, inside and out you shall overlay it, and shall make on it a molding of gold all around. You shall cast four rings of gold for it, and put them in its four corners; two rings shall be on one side, and two rings on the other side. And you shall make poles of acacia wood, and overlay them with gold. You shall put the poles into the rings on the sides of the ark, that the ark may be carried by them. The poles shall be in the rings of the ark; they shall not be taken from it. And you shall put into the ark the Testimony which I will give you."

Exodus 26:1-6, 15-25 says,

Moreover you shall make the tabernacle with ten curtains of fine woven linen and blue, purple, and scarlet thread; with artistic designs of cherubim you shall weave them. The length of each curtain shall be twenty-eight cubits, and the width of each curtain four cubits. And every one of the curtains shall have the same measurements. Five curtains shall be coupled to one another, and the other five curtains shall be coupled to one another. And you shall make loops of blue yarn on the edge of the curtain on the selvedge of one set, and likewise you shall do on the outer edge of the other curtain of the second set. Fifty loops you shall make in the one curtain, and fifty loops you shall make on the edge of the curtain that is on the end of the second set, that the loops may be clasped to one another. And you shall make fifty clasps of gold, and couple the curtains together with the clasps, so that it may be one tabernacle... "And for the tabernacle you shall make the boards of acacia wood, standing upright. Ten cubits shall be the length of a board, and a cubit and a half shall be the width of each board. Two tenons shall be in each board for binding one to another. Thus you shall make for all the boards of the tabernacle. And you shall make the boards for the tabernacle, twenty boards for the south side. You shall make forty sockets of silver under the twenty boards: two sockets under each of the boards for its two tenons. And for the second side of the tabernacle, the north side, there shall be twenty boards and their forty sockets of silver: two sockets under each of the boards. For *the far side of the tabernacle, westward, you shall make six boards. And you shall also make two boards for the two back corners of the tabernacle. They shall be coupled together at the bottom and they shall be coupled together at the top by one ring. Thus it shall be for both of them. They shall be for the two corners. So there shall be eight boards with their sockets of silver—sixteen sockets—two sockets under each of the boards.*

Our third builder commissioned in this trio of heavenly blueprint builders was King David. David was given the blueprint for the Temple, however, he had to pass it on to Solomon his son, and hence it was called the Temple of Solomon. David had disobeyed God and was considered a bloody man of war and thereby unfit to build. You could read the account in 1 Chronicles chapters 17, 22, 28-29. Here is a snippet of the text again for reference:

1 Chronicles 28:2-19 says,

Then King David rose to his feet and said, "Hear me, my brethren and my people: I had it in my heart to build a house of rest for the ark of the covenant of the LORD, and for the footstool of our God, and had made preparations to build it. But God said to me, 'You shall not build a house for My name, because you have been a man of war and have shed blood.' However the LORD God of Israel chose me above all the house of my father to be king over Israel forever, for He has chosen Judah to be the ruler. And of the house of Judah, the house of my father, and among the sons of my father, He was pleased with me to make me king over all Israel. And of all my sons (for the LORD has given me many sons) He has chosen my son Solomon to sit on the throne of the kingdom of the LORD over Israel. Now He said to me, 'It is your son Solomon who shall build My house and My courts; for I have chosen him to be My son, and I will be his Father. Moreover I will establish his kingdom forever, if he is steadfast to observe My commandments and My judgments, as it is this day.' Now therefore, in the sight of all Israel, the assembly of the LORD, and in the hearing of our God, be careful to seek out all the commandments of the LORD your God, that you may possess this good land, and leave it as an inheritance for your children after you forever. "As for you, my son Solomon, know the God of your father, and serve Him with a loyal heart and with a willing mind; for the LORD searches all hearts and understands all the intent of the thoughts. If you seek Him, He will be found by you; but if you forsake Him, He will cast you off forever. Consider now, for the LORD has chosen you to build a house for the sanctuary; be strong, and do it." Then David gave his son Solomon the plans for the vestibule, its houses, its treasuries, its upper chambers, its inner chambers, and the place of the mercy seat; and the plans for all that he had by the Spirit, of the courts of the house of the LORD, of all the chambers all around, of the treasuries of the house of God, and of the treasuries for the dedicated things; also for the division of the priests and the Levites, for all the work of the service of the house of the LORD, and for all the articles of service in the house of the LORD. He gave gold by weight for things of gold, for all articles used in every kind of service; also silver for all articles of silver by weight, for all articles used in every kind of service; the weight for the lampstands of gold, and their lamps of gold, by weight for each lampstand and its lamps; for the lampstands of silver by weight, for the lampstand and its lamps, according to the use of each lampstand. And by weight he gave gold for the tables of the showbread, for each table, and silver for the tables of silver; also pure gold for the forks, the basins, the pitchers of pure gold, and the golden bowls—he gave gold by weight for every bowl; and for the silver bowls, silver by weight for every bowl; and refined gold by weight for the altar of incense, and for the construction of the chariot, that is, the gold cherubim that spread their wings and overshadowed the ark of the covenant of the LORD. "All this," said David, "the LORD made me understand in writing, by His hand upon me, all the works of these plans."

These projects were not small undertakings. They were elaborate and well laid out in their specifications and blueprints. God spoke directly to the builder and specified every last detail. In the natural, the same actions must happen when you want to build something. First you must have a blueprint and hire the qualified person(s) to lead the building of the project, and then you build.

The natural order to build an earthly edifice applies to the spiritual realm where the builder must be qualified and ready to build the way God wishes it to be built and not according to some earthly, fleshly design or desire put forth by a planning committee or a church board. It must not be adulterated in any way and substandard materials must not be used.

Hence, the designated person(s) is needed to lead this building project for the complete restoration of Zion! And God in His wisdom has appointed Apostles and Prophets as the wise master builders who receive and understand by revelation the building blueprints from Heaven. Bear in mind that these Apostles and Prophets need to be submitted to God and walking in transparency with the grace of God upon them, not just to seek fame and notoriety. If a person is not called to these offices, they will never build anything with substance or longevity.

One of the problems that we face with modern-day churches is that most of them are being built according to "a denominational blueprint or model." We have a variety of blueprints, but the question that needs to be asked is, how many of them are being built according to the Blueprint from Heaven? Knowing that Heaven's Blueprint is released to Apostles and Prophets through the vehicle of divine revelation, is this being correctly discerned? Some mega-churches have been built after the denominational plan and have gone into receivership and loss because the vision for building was human and personal, and not imparted from Heaven. This could be an indication of an indiscriminate leader not seeking after God's divine blueprint, but rather seeking after the approval of man and the congregation.

To bring further understanding to this, let us look at a few portions of Scripture.

The Scriptures reveal that on a particular day as Jesus and His disciples (Apostles in training) came to the region of Caesarea Philippi, (Matthew 16:13) He asked them one of the most notable questions in all of His dealings with them up to that time. In the following passage of Scripture, Jesus Christ asks His disciples the pointed question, *"Who do people say the Son of Man is?"* And more noteworthy even is the question He posed to them; *"Who do you say that I am?* (correctly answered by Peter!) These questions seem strange after He conscripted all of the disciples who left behind their occupations/families/daily oblations to whole-heartedly follow Him. However, in order to understand where I am going with this, we need to read on: Here is what Matthew 16:13-26 says,

When Jesus came to the region of Caesarea Philippi, he asked his disciples, "Who do people say the Son of Man is?" They replied, "Some say John the Baptist; others say Elijah; and still others, Jeremiah or one of the prophets." "But what about you?" he asked. "Who do you say I am?" Simon Peter answered, "You are the Christ, the Son of the living God." Jesus replied, "Blessed are you, Simon son of Jonah, for this was not revealed to you by man, but by my Father in Heaven. And I tell you that you are Peter, and on this rock I will build my Church, and the gates of Hades will not overcome it. I will give you the keys of the kingdom of Heaven; whatever you bind on earth will be bound in Heaven, and whatever you loose on earth will be loosed in Heaven." Then he warned his disciples not to tell anyone that he was the Christ. From that time on Jesus began to explain to his disciples that he must go to Jerusalem and suffer many things at the hands of the elders, chief priests and teachers of the law, and that he must be killed and on the third day be raised to life. Peter took him aside and began to rebuke him. "Never, Lord!" he said. "This shall never happen to you!" Jesus turned and said to Peter, "Get behind me, Satan! You are a stumbling block to me; you do not have in mind the things of God, but the things of men." Then Jesus said to his disciples, "If anyone would come after me, he must deny himself and take up his cross and follow me. For whoever wants to save his life will lose it, but whoever loses his life for me will find it. What good will it be for a man if he gains the whole world, yet forfeits his soul? Or what can a man give in exchange for his soul?"

Jesus was trying the hearts of His disciples. He wanted to know how they felt about Him and what heartfelt convictions they carried regarding Him. He wanted to make sure they were not just coasting on the bandwagon of novelty with tickling ears. This to me is very powerful! Remember that this is Jesus Christ; the Man who knew what was in the hearts of all men. He was the Man Sent From God, and yet He prodded His disciples to answer a seemingly redundant question in wanting to know the depth of conviction in their hearts regarding Him!

This was indeed a loaded question and Jesus Christ as The Apostle of all Apostles had to be sure that they themselves were convinced beyond the shadow of a doubt as to Who He was. He certainly knew Who He was. Jesus Christ had the God confidence of knowing who He was and He knew His purpose as well as His Source. The Apostles' response to that question began to reveal a sad lack of revelation knowledge of Who He really was. "Some say John the Baptist; others say Elijah; and still others, Jeremiah or one of the prophets;" were some of their answers. Then out of the mouth of Peter came the following: "You are the Christ, the Son of The Living God"; and with great elation Jesus Christ declared that the source of Peter's revelation was not from flesh and blood but that he had indeed heard from His Father who was in Heaven.

Jesus declared to him, *"flesh and blood did not reveal this to you."* The Greek word translated as *reveal* in English is the word *apokalupto* from which we get our English word *apocalypse* which signifies *to uncover, unveilment of all things.* Only one person out of the twelve was hearing from God that day and it was Peter!

Peter's name in the Greek meant little rock and Jesus Christ said to him, "you are known as little rock, however, upon the *Big Rock* of this revelation that you just received I will be building My Church and the gates of hell will not be able to prevail against It!"

This was the very first time in the New Testament or during Jesus' time on the earth that He referred to His building of The Church, which referred to people, not to stones or bricks. Up to that time all He spoke about was The Kingdom of God and now He introduces this brand new concept of The Church.

We see the Church being launched in power in Acts chapter 2:1-3, as the Holy Spirit descends upon the Apostles and the other Saints that were gathered in the *upper room* on the eventful Day of Pentecost. From this point on, there were great signs, wonders and miracles arising out of a powerfully preached Jesus Christ.

Jesus Christ was very particular in ensuring that His Church, that He emphatically said He would build, was launched accurately. The early Apostles and Saints had to wait in the *upper room*. Think about how trying this must have been. They were involved in a series of great occurrences and miracles and now they had to wait for the Promise that the Holy

Spirit would be released to ensure that Jesus Christ's full mandate would be carried out on the earth.

This same care and attention was used by Jesus Christ when He called His disciples and asked them that powerful question—*"who do you say that I, the Son of Man am?"* I believe that He wanted to ensure that the ones He was going to use in laying the foundation of His Church were indeed worthy.

All the Apostles answered incorrectly with their "some say you are_____" except for Apostle Peter who declared to Jesus that He was *"The Christ, The Son of The Living God!"* Jesus Christ perceived that only a True Son of God could have known this. He told Peter that what he (Peter) spoke came by revelation and not from within himself. And it was this revelation from Father God that He (Jesus Christ) was going to build the Church upon. I believe that Peter's correct answer gave Jesus Christ the assurance that He could go to the Cross and give up His life so that the Church could be born.

The *upper room* experience heralded the arrival of the Holy Spirit on earth to build the Church. On that eventful day, only Apostle Peter was used to bring clarity as to what was taking place! It was a cacophony of news and many of the onlookers thought they were all drunk and disorderly at 9 o'clock in the morning.

Acts 2:14-16 says,

Then Peter stood up with the Eleven, raised his voice and addressed the crowd: "Fellow Jews and all of you who live in Jerusalem, let me explain this to you; listen carefully to what I say. These men are not drunk, as you suppose. It's only nine in the morning! No, this is what was spoken by the prophet Joel:"

Now, don't get me wrong, as was said earlier—one of the problems that we face today with churches is that most of them are being built according to "a denominational blueprint or model." We have a variety of blueprints, but the question that needs to be asked is how many of them are being built according to the Blueprint from Heaven when it is clear in Scripture that Heaven's Blueprint is released to Apostles and Prophets through the vehicle of divine revelation. *Many functioning under this mantle possess some truth* and some of them are very sincere. However, a lot of them are building according to tradition and the patterns of men, building through natural vision and not by revelation. After all, a nice, new, big building might be impressive in the eyes of man, and for reasons of "building a ministry" as space is needed. It is human, fallible and rather an easy path to follow, rather than to seek out the plans from Father God. It has led to building mausoleum type churches with huge debt where the sheep are not fed and cared for.

The Bible clearly says that the natural man cannot receive the things of the Spirit (see 1 Corinthians 2:14).

Allow me to say this to you: I believe that the pattern we need to fashion in this day and age is what we see in the building of the Tabernacle of David. It is the one that the Lord said He would have restored in the last days of the Old Covenant or the last days of Israel, according to Amos 9 and Acts 15:16-17. Jesus came and sat on the throne of David. David was a man after God's own heart and his tabernacle held and continues to hold great importance and significance, which we will delve into.

Amos 9:11 says,

On that day I will raise up The tabernacle of David, which has fallen down, And repair its damages; I will raise up its ruins, And rebuild it as in the days of old;

Acts 15:16-17 says,

After this I will return And will rebuild the tabernacle of David, which has fallen down; I will rebuild its ruins, And I will set it up; So that the rest of mankind may seek the LORD, Even all the Gentiles who are called by My name, Says the LORD who does all these things.

I believe when David built that tent and placed the Ark of the Covenant under it where continuous Praise and Worship billowed up to Heaven, he captured the Heart of God. And David accomplished this by direct revelation. When God looked upon this heartfelt worship He spoke from Heaven saying that this is what He had been looking for, it was a sweet-smelling savour in His nostrils.

1 Chronicles 16:1-6, 37-42 says,

So they brought the ark of God, and set it in the midst of the tabernacle that David had erected for it. Then they offered burnt offerings and peace offerings before God. And when David had finished offering the burnt offerings and the peace offerings, he blessed the people in the name of the LORD. Then he distributed to everyone of Israel, both man and woman, to everyone a loaf of bread, a piece of meat, and a cake of raisins. And he appointed some of the Levites to minister before the ark of the LORD, to commemorate, to thank, and to praise the LORD God of Israel: Asaph the chief, and next to him Zechariah, then Jeiel, Shemiramoth, Jehiel, Mattithiah, Eliab, Benaiah, and Obed-Edom: Jeiel with stringed instruments and harps, but Asaph made music with cymbals; Benaiah and Jahaziel the priests regularly blew the trumpets before the ark of the covenant of God. ... So he left Asaph and his brothers there before the ark of the covenant of the LORD to minister before the ark regularly, as every day's work required; and Obed-Edom with his sixty-eight brethren, including Obed-Edom the son of Jeduthun, and Hosah, to be gatekeepers; and Zadok the priest and his brethren the priests, before the tabernacle of the LORD at the high place that was at Gibeon, to offer burnt offerings to the LORD on the altar of burnt offering regularly morning and evening, and to do according to all that is written in the Law of the LORD which He commanded Israel; and with them Heman and Jeduthun and the rest who were chosen, who were designated by name, to give thanks to the LORD, because His mercy endures forever; and with them Heman and Jeduthun, to sound aloud with trumpets and cymbals and the musical instruments of God. Now the sons of Jeduthun were gatekeepers.

I find it most interesting that the depth of the revelation concerning praise and worship does not come from the New Testament but it comes from the Old Testament—especially the book of Psalms, which was mostly penned by the hand of David.

For example most of the words that we use to understand Praise and Worship are all Hebrew words, such as:

• Tehillah: psalm, praise.

• Halal: to praise, celebrate with dancing, glory, sing (praise), boast.

- Todhah: confession, thanksgiving,—(fruit of our lips giving thanks to God).
- Shabhach: to praise, glorify.
- Zamar or Yadhah: to stretch out the hand, confess.

And the Greek word
- Doxa: glory, by praise.

True praise and worship is not a set played by a group of gifted musicians with an incredible musical arrangement and an array of voices that would make you tremble. Please know this, that true praise and worship begins in the heart and because the heart becomes so overwhelmed and excited, it needs to fully express itself.

Then out of the abundance of the HEART the MOUTH begins to speak fervent praises to our Heavenly King, but even that is inadequate, as the words do not fully express what the heart wants to say! The overflow includes shouting, clapping, dancing and a host of other things to express the praise in our hearts, which fail to fully extol God's greatness! But because He is God, He understands what we are offering as praise to Him, be it words, songs or dancing.

Some churches look down upon all the clapping, and shouting and dancing and all of the musical instruments. The early Christian denominations did not allow musical instruments. When the various religious denominations were formed, many of their leaders opposed the use of mechanical instruments in worship. Here are some of their quotes:

"The organ in the worship of God is an ensign of Baal" (Martin Luther, reformer and founder of the Lutheran Church).

"Musical instruments in celebrating the praises of God would be no more suitable than the burning of incense, the lighting of lamps, and the restoration of the other shadows of the law. The Papists, therefore, have foolishly borrowed this, as well as many other things, from the Jews" (John Calvin, founder of the Presbyterian Church).

"I have no objections to the instrument in our chapels, provided they are neither heard nor seen" (John Wesley, founder of the Methodist Church).

"I am an old man and a minister; and I declare that I have never known them to be productive of any good in the worship of God; and I have reason to believe that they were productive of much evil. Music as a science I admire and esteem, but instruments of music in the House of God, I abominate and abhor. This is the abuse of music; and here I register my protest against all such corruptions in the worship of the Author of Christianity who requires His followers to worship Him in spirit and in truth" (Adam Clarke, Methodist scholar and commentator).

Charles Spurgeon, one of the greatest Baptist preachers ever, quoted 1 Corinthians 14:15 and added, "I would as soon pray to God with machinery as to sing to God with machinery."

The Old Testament Children of God lavished worship and praises on Father God. They set the pattern as to how we should worship and with times progressing into what they became at the end of the Old Testament and the beginning of the New, many churches grew in their beliefs that lavish worship, loud worship, harps, cymbals and flutes had no place in the worship service. They believed that We the Believers in the present are called to build according to the New Covenant which relegates it all to a bland, methodical form of worship, and even better without instruments according to the early founders of our modern denominations, often quoting Colossians 3:16 *"Let the message of Christ dwell among you richly as you teach and admonish one another with all wisdom through psalms, hymns, and songs from the Spirit, singing to God with gratitude in your hearts."*

Because the Scriptures did not mention instruments, the Denominationalists took it to mean that worship should be devoid of all musical instruments; not a piano, not an organ, not a flute.

But the Old Testament was the blueprint with the patterns of worship needed in this present day. So to the New Covenant style of worship devoid of mechanical instruments, and only having song for expression, I say, "baloney" as God Himself by His Spirit revealed to us in the book of Acts that He was going to restore the Tabernacle of David.

A very interesting characteristic about the Tabernacle of David was the following: David built this tent and put the Ark under it but he failed to put a veil to separate it from onlookers as prescribed under Old Testament law. Here is a portion of Scripture, which tells us the specifications of the temple originally built with a veil separating the Holy Place from the Most Holy Place:

Exodus 26:30-33 says,

And you shall raise up the tabernacle according to its pattern which you were shown on the mountain. "You shall make a veil woven of blue, purple, and scarlet thread, and fine woven linen. It shall be woven with an artistic design of cherubim. You shall hang it upon the four pillars of acacia wood overlaid with gold. Their hooks shall be gold, upon four sockets of silver. ³³ And you shall hang the veil from the clasps. Then you shall bring the ark of the Testimony in there, behind the veil. The veil shall be a divider for you between the holy place and the Most Holy."

David's Temple – 2 Samuel 6:14-18 says,

Then David danced before the LORD with all his might; and David was wearing a linen ephod. So David and all the house of Israel brought up the ark of the LORD with shouting and with the sound of the trumpet. Now as the ark of the LORD came into the City of David, Michal, Saul's daughter, looked through a window and saw King David leaping and whirling before the LORD; and she despised him in her heart. So they brought the ark of the LORD, and set it in its place in the midst of the tabernacle that David had erected for it. Then David offered burnt offerings and peace offerings before the LORD. And when David had finished offering burnt offerings and peace offerings, he blessed the people in the name of the LORD of hosts.

David, who was obviously in the will of God, erected a tent in which people worshipped joyfully without being separated from the Ark of the Covenant by the Veil.

Remember that the Veil in the Temple was torn in two when Jesus died on the Cross (Matthew 27:51). Clearly, this tent or tabernacle had great prophetic significance for Believers back in the 1ST Century and also today as it did not adhere to the pattern of the old temple, and was a symbol of things to come.

Hebrews 12:18-24 explains this difference in the worship beautifully. Here is what it says,

For you have not come to the mountain that may be touched and that burned with fire, and to blackness and darkness and tempest, and the sound of a trumpet and the voice of words, so that those who heard it begged that the word should not be spoken to them anymore. (For they could not endure what was commanded: "And if so much as a beast touches the mountain, it shall be stoned or shot with an arrow." And so terrifying was the sight that Moses said, "I am exceedingly afraid and trembling.") But you have come to Mount Zion and to the city of the living God, the heavenly Jerusalem, to an innumerable company of angels, to the general assembly and church of the firstborn who are registered in heaven, to God the Judge of all, to the spirits of just men made perfect, to Jesus the Mediator of the new covenant, and to the blood of sprinkling that speaks better things than that of Abel." (See Exodus chapter 19 as a reference)

The Lord absolutely loved this because David was operating solely by revelation and he stepped into the reality of the New Covenant, into the time Jesus was crucified and the veil in the Temple was rent from TOP to bottom; signifying that it was not man that tore it but God, Himself! HALLELUJAH, David saw that and flowed in it by revelation!

David entered into this by faith, the finished work of Calvary (remember Jesus was the Lamb that was slain before the very foundations of the earth—in the mind of God it was already done). He brought the people into a time when we would be all kings and priests unto God and that there would be no veil separating us!

I submit to you that David was a type of a New Testament Apostle and he was a pioneer living ahead of his time. He was "sent" (apostello) by God as a forerunner to accomplish all this; hence the need for Apostles and Prophets being raised up in every region.

We need to build according to the pattern of David because the Tabernacle of David is being restored. We need that Davidic spirit and anointing; that spirit which is fearless that wants the Lord to be glorified and exalted and that wants the enemies of the Lord crushed and defeated.

Hear me I believe that Psalm 132:8 must be the cry of every true leader, Believer, and local church! We are not aiming to build something that God visits but where He can come and REST, STAY, LIVE!!! That is why most of the moves of God that we see come and go because they build a place where God can come to visit but not rest in! True rest only comes when you are home! Are you hearing me, you can travel all over the world but there is nothing like coming HOME!!! Rest and home are synonymous for the weary traveller!

That word REST means COMFORTABLE! God wants to be COMFORTABLE; He wants to REST in our churches!

CHAPTER FOUR
GOD'S RESTING PLACE

REST WAS VERY VITAL IN GOD'S CREATIVE PROCESS. REST MEANS TO CEASE FROM labour and toil, as when God rested on the seventh day...

Genesis 2:1-3 says,

Thus the heavens and the earth, and all the host of them, were finished. And on the seventh day God ended His work, which He had done, and He rested on the seventh day from all His work, which He had done. Then God blessed the seventh day and sanctified it, because in it He rested from all His work, which God had created and made.

It was on the seventh day; God's day of rest that He spoke to Adam and Eve and revealed His heart to them... It was when God rested that Adam and Eve began to work. Remember that Adam and Eve were created on the sixth day of God's creative process as such Adam's first day was God's seventh in which He (God) rested and Adam began to do what they were created to do.

I believe that as we build churches where God can come and REST that we would see signs, wonders, miracles, conversions, and salvations. There will be a Move of God in our cities wherever a place for God is built! You see the power of conviction becomes so strong in the place where

God's Presence Dwells. It is like what happened in the book of Acts... Here are few accounts that we must consider, which I would list in several categories:

INDIVIDUAL MIRACLES IN THE BOOK OF ACTS

RESURRECTIONS FROM THE DEAD
1. Apostle Peter raises the disciple Tabitha—9:36-42
2. Apostle Paul raises the young man Eutychus—20:9-12

MIRACULOUS CURES
1. Apostle Peter heals the lame man at the Temple gate—3:1-16
2. Apostle Peter heals the paralytic Aeneas—9:33-35
3. Apostle Paul cures the lame man of Lystra—14:7-9
4. Apostle Paul stoned and miraculously healed at Lystra—14:19
5. Apostle Paul exorcises girl possessed of divining spirit—16:16-18
6. Apostle Paul heals Publius' father of dysentery—28:7-8

MIRACULOUS PENALTIES OR AFFLICTIONS ON SEVERAL
1. Ananias and Sapphira were struck dead at Apostle Peter's feet—5:5-11
2. Saul struck blind on the road to Damascus—9:8-9
3. Herod suddenly slain by an angel—12:23
4. Apostle Paul temporarily blinds the sorcerer Elymas—13:9-12

NATURE OR COSMIC MIRACLES
1. Violent wind at the Cenacle in Jerusalem—2:2-6
2. Shaking of the assembly building in Jerusalem—4:31
3. Prison doors open for the Apostles—5:17-25
4. Philip snatched by the Spirit of the Lord—8:39
5. Apostle Peter liberated from prison by an angel—12:5-11
6. Chains fall from Apostles Paul and Silas—16:25-30
7. Apostle Paul shakes off viper from his arm—28:3-6

COLLECTIVE MIRACLE SITUATIONS IN THE BOOK OF ACTS
1. Many signs and wonders done by the Apostles in Jerusalem—2:43
2. Apostles perform signs and wonders among the people—5:12

3. Apostle Peter's shadow cures many in the streets—5:15
4. Multitudes from outside Jerusalem are healed—5:16
5. Stephen works great signs and wonders—6:8
6. Phillip cures crippled and possessed in Samaria—8:6-8, 13
7. Miracles worked by Apostles Paul and Barnabas on mission journey—14:3
8. Great signs and wonders done among the Gentiles—15:12
9. Miracles worked through objects touched by Paul—19:11-12
10. Apostle Paul heals all the sick brought to him on Malta—28:9

I believe that all those miracles took place because they built according to what God wanted—Jesus told them to wait in Jerusalem until the Holy Spirit came and then begin to build and they did that and BANG; the Lord showed up!

God is looking for a place to rest! He doesn't want to be just a visitor!

Psalm 132:13-14 now these are key verses—Here God is saying that it is He who has chosen Zion to be His resting place FOREVER! Here is what is says,

For the Lord has chosen Zion, He has desired it for His dwelling place: "This is My resting place forever; Here I will dwell, for I have desired it."

• He Desired a place to Rest
• He has chosen to rest in Zion Forever.
• This was not only for David's time and generation...

What does Zion represent; why has God chosen it for the place of His Rest Forever?

David rose to the position of King and what he did when it happened presents to us a wonderful picture of the Church that the Lord desires. 2 Samuel 5:1-10 says,

Then all the tribes of Israel came to David at Hebron and spoke, saying, "Indeed we are your bone and your flesh. Also, in time past, when Saul was king over us, you were the one who led Israel out

and brought them in; and the LORD said to you, 'You shall shepherd My people Israel, and be ruler over Israel.'" Therefore all the elders of Israel came to the king at Hebron, and King David made a covenant with them at Hebron before the LORD. And they anointed David king over Israel. David was thirty years old when he began to reign, and he reigned forty years. In Hebron he reigned over Judah seven years and six months, and in Jerusalem he reigned thirty-three years over all Israel and Judah. And the king and his men went to Jerusalem against the Jebusites, the inhabitants of the land, who spoke to David, saying, "You shall not come in here; but the blind and the lame will repel you," thinking, "David cannot come in here." Nevertheless David took the stronghold of Zion (that is, the City of David). Now David said on that day, "Whoever climbs up by way of the water shaft and defeats the Jebusites (the lame and the blind, who are hated by David's soul), he shall be chief and captain." Therefore they say, "The blind and the lame shall not come into the house." Then David dwelt in the stronghold, and called it the City of David. And David built all around from the Millo and inward. So David went on and became great, and the LORD God of hosts was with him."

At this point, David was King over Judah where he had reigned seven and a half years. Saul had died, and the prophetic word that Samuel had given to him some twenty-three years before, is about to be fulfilled. However, he dwelt in Hebron for seven and a half years before the word came to pass. Hebron is a very powerful place in the plan of God for our lives.

CHAPTER FIVE
HEBRON

ALTHOUGH HEBRON WAS A PHYSICAL CITY, IT CARRIES A POWERFUL SPIRITUAL dimension in God. It can represent the following: Hebron in the Hebrew is translated—confederacy, from which the noun confederate, is derived, and carries the following meaning—To unite in a confederacy or to be united in a league. So from this we can derive that *Hebron* represented a place of unity.

Remember the children of Israel's journey from Egypt to the Promised Land? The first encounter they had with truly walking in unity came about forty days after they left Egypt and Moses sent out the twelve spies. This is what happened:

Numbers 13:1-3, 17-23, 26-33 says,

And the LORD spoke to Moses, saying, "Send men to spy out the land of Canaan, which I am giving to the children of Israel; from each tribe of their fathers you shall send a man, every one a leader among them." So Moses sent them from the Wilderness of Paran according to the command of the LORD, all of them men who were heads of the children of Israel. ... Then Moses sent them to spy out the land of Canaan, and said to them, "Go up this way into the South, and go up to the mountains, and see what the land is like: whether the people who dwell in it are strong or weak, few or many; whether the land they dwell in is good or bad; whether the cities they inhabit are like camps or strongholds; whether the land is rich or poor; and whether there are forests there or not. Be of good courage. And bring some of the fruit of the land." Now the time was the season of the first ripe grapes. So they went up and spied out the land from the Wilderness of Zin as far as Rehob, near the entrance of Hamath. And they went up through the South and came to Hebron; *Ahiman, Sheshai, and Talmai, the descendants of Anak, were there. (Now Hebron was built seven years before Zoan in Egypt.) Then they came to the Valley of Eshcol, and there cut down a branch with one cluster of grapes; they carried it between two of them on a pole. They also brought some of the pomegranates and figs. ... Now they departed and came back to Moses and Aaron and all the congregation of the children of Israel in the Wilderness of Paran, at Kadesh; they brought back word to them and to all the congregation, and showed them the fruit of the land. Then they told him, and said: "We went to the land where you sent us. It truly flows with milk and honey, and this is its fruit. Nevertheless the people who dwell in the land are strong; the cities are fortified and very large; moreover we saw the descendants of Anak there. The Amalekites dwell in the land of the South; the Hittites, the Jebusites, and the Amorites dwell in the mountains; and the Canaanites dwell by the sea and along the banks of the Jordan."* Then Caleb quieted the people before Moses, and said, "Let us go up at once and take possession, for we are well able to overcome it." *But the men who had gone up with him said, "We are not able to go up against the people, for they are stronger than we." And they gave the children of Israel a bad report of the land which they had spied out, saying, "The land through which we have gone as spies is a land that devours its inhabitants, and all the people whom we saw in it are men of great stature.* There we saw the giants (the descendants of Anak came from the giants); and we were like grasshoppers in our own sight, *and so we were in their sight."*

1. They entered through the south where Hebron was and they came upon the sons of Anak; *giants*, and ten came back with an evil

report that they could not take the land. They saw themselves as *grasshoppers*! Only Joshua and Caleb (whose names meant "Praise & Worship" and "Doubly Fruitful") came back with a good report.

2. They went to the place of *unity* and came back divided, and for forty years wandered through the wilderness before the Lord killed out the "unbelievers", the ones that fostered disunity (Numbers 14:26-38). Only Joshua and Caleb remained, and a whole *new generation* was raised up to go in with them.

3. After forty years they are about to enter the Promised Land; however, this time they do not enter from the south but from the north – entirely in the opposite direction – and the first place that they encountered was Jericho (see Joshua chapters 2 and 6), and the last place they came to was Hebron (see Joshua chapter 14).

4. I believe that "Hebron" could also represent one of the final frontiers for the Church [according to Ephesians 4:3-6].

Here are some of the other dimensions of Heron that I believe are very valuable to us as the Church today!

1. It is a place of separation from earthbound Christianity into one's true destiny and purpose—Abraham visited that place and entered into his true purpose after he separated from Lot his cousin—see Genesis 13.

2. It is the place of a name change—Abram was changed to Abraham, and Sari was changed to Sarah in Hebron—see Genesis 13:18.

3. It is a place of declared destiny, a place of *transition* into a higher realm: even though Abraham dwelt there, he was still looking for a city whose maker and builder was God—In essence he was looking for the Church.

David also had a powerful time of his life in Hebron. David was in a place of transition, as Samuel had prophesied over him some twenty-three years before, that the Lord had chosen him to lead his people Israel. He got his first anointing in his earthly father's house (see 1 Samuel 16:1); he received his second anointing in Hebron (see 2 Samuel 2:4); and now he is receiving his third anointing that will take him into his ultimate purpose—to lead all of God's people (see 2 Samuel 5).

It was here that David made a *Covenant* with Leadership—2 Samuel 5:1-3 says,

> *Then all the tribes of Israel came to David at Hebron and spoke, saying, "Indeed we are your bone and your flesh. Also, in time past, when Saul was king over us, you were the one who led Israel out and brought them in; and the LORD said to you, 'You shall shepherd My people Israel, and be ruler over Israel.'" Therefore all the elders of Israel came to the king at Hebron, and King David made a covenant with them at Hebron before the LORD. And they anointed David king over Israel."*

This third anointing pushes us to the ultimate—it is similar to the anointing by *fire* (see Malachi 3:1-3 and Mathew 3:11-12)—it is the place of serious commitment.

It was from Hebron, and after his third anointing, that David rises up to take the *stronghold of Zion*—he could not continue to live his life in transition—this was the real deal; this is what he was born for. However, as we would see, there is always confrontation to the purpose of God.

The Blind and the Lame – 2 Samuel 5:6-10 says,

> *And the king and his men went to Jerusalem against the Jebusites, the inhabitants of the land, who spoke to David, saying, "You shall not come in here; but the blind and the lame will repel you," thinking, "David cannot come in here." Nevertheless David took the stronghold of Zion (that is, the City of David). Now David said on that day, "Whoever climbs up by way of the water shaft and defeats the Jebusites (the lame and the blind, who are hated by David's soul), he shall be chief and captain." Therefore they say, "The blind and the lame shall not come into the house." Then David dwelt in the stronghold, and called it the City of David. And David built all around from the Millo and inward. So David went on and became great, and the LORD God of hosts was with him."*

The word for lame in the Hebrew is translated HESITANT—people that refuse to function in a forceful way—*"From the days of John the Baptist until now, the kingdom of heaven has been subjected to violence, and violent people have been raiding it."* Matthew 11:12 NIV—*passivity does not advance the Kingdom of God!* It only locks us into religious activity. David destroyed the lame and the blind—the Word declares that they were hated of David's soul. He then goes on and establishes *Zion* (a type of the Church), as a place of *dominion* for God's people! This was very prophetic as he was proclaiming what the Church should be like in the earth.

Let me submit this to you, I believe that God is seeking for this same attitude today as we build. He is seeking for those who would have that "Davidic" spirit. One that will not compromise. One that will not settle for the hesitant to rule them.

To build a "Zion Church" we must possess the Davidic spirit and anointing. David was very militant and he was indeed a warrior. He was also a worshipper, he was also a builder, and he moved both in his priestly and kingly anointing...

I like what A.W. Tozer said, and I quote:

"The church has surrendered her once lofty concept of God and has substituted for it one so low, so ignoble, as to be utterly unworthy of thinking, worshipping men. Not deliberately, but little by little, without her knowledge; and her very unawareness only makes her situation all the more tragic."

Like I said before, Zion was originally an ancient Jebusite fortress in the city of Jerusalem. After David's conquest of the fortress, Jerusalem became a possession of Israel. The royal palace was built there, and Zion/Jerusalem became the seat of power in Israel's kingdom.

Zion never lost its ability to be a fortress; only it was in the wrong hands. God still desires for His Church to be a fortress in the earth. A place where many can go and find help. A place where they can be built up to become everything that God intended! Let us have a look at this Church.

CHAPTER SIX
THE MT. ZION CHURCH

NOW THAT WE HAVE ESTABLISHED THOUGH SCRIPTURE THAT ZION IS NO LONGER A city, fortress, or the physical Jerusalem, we will now explore the Church as it is meant to be in this age.

As we move forward with this chapter, allow me to say this: unless we are converted and become as little children we do not truly enter or live the Kingdom life! We read in Matthew 18:2-3, which says,

> *Then Jesus called a little child to Him, set him in the midst of them, and said, "Assuredly, I say to you, unless you are converted and become as little children, you will by no means enter the kingdom of heaven."*

What is so powerful about this statement is this; a child has not as yet been able to form an opinion on life or issues. However, most of us accepted Christ and His salvation as adults or young adults with pre-formed opinions on life's issues. These pre-existing opinions need the conversion experience in order to make us into the new creatures that the Bible refers to as those who have had old things pass away, all things made new.

DYNAMICS OF THE MT. ZION/FORTRESS CHURCH
Isaiah 2:1-4 says,

This is what Isaiah son of Amoz saw concerning Judah and Jerusalem: *In the last days the mountain of the Lord's temple will be established as the highest of the mountains; it will be exalted above the hills, and all nations will stream to it. Many peoples will come and say, "Come, let us go up to the mountain of the Lord,* to the temple of the God of Jacob. He will teach us his ways, so that we may walk in his paths." *The law will go out from Zion, the word of the Lord from Jerusalem.* He will judge between the nations and will settle disputes for many peoples. *They will beat their swords into plowshares and their spears into pruning hooks.* Nation will not take up sword against nation, nor will they train for war anymore. (NIV)

Psalm 48, which says,

Great is the LORD, *and most worthy of praise, in the city of our God, his holy mountain. Beautiful in its loftiness, the joy of the whole earth, like the heights of Zaphon is Mount Zion, the city of the Great King. God is in her citadels;* he has shown himself to be her fortress. When the kings joined forces, when they advanced together, they saw her and were astounded; they fled in terror. Trembling seized them there, pain like that of a woman in labour. *You destroyed them like ships of Tarshish shattered by an east wind.* As we have heard, so we have seen *in the city of the* LORD *Almighty, in the city of our God: God makes her secure forever. Within your temple, O God, we meditate on your unfailing love. Like your name, O God, your praise reaches to the ends of the earth; your right hand is filled with righteousness.* Mount Zion rejoices, the villages of Judah are glad because of your judgments. *Walk about Zion, go around her, count her towers, consider well her ramparts, view her citadels,* that you may tell of them to the next generation. *For this God is our God for ever and ever; he will be our guide even to the end.* (NIV)

God is Great in the Fortress Church and worthy of all praise. It is beautiful in its *loftiness* or *elevation*.

PRINCIPLE ONE—LOFTINESS PSALM 48:1

Loftiness—this word is not used in the sense of being proud or haughty but it is to be used to denote position or situation; a place of elevation.

Mt. Zion, which we have established, clearly is a type of the Church and it is beautiful because of its *elevation, its loftiness, and its position*! As a matter of fact, the terminology "Mt. Zion on the sides of the North" in Hebrew depicts *Elevation or Height*.

Elevation or Height is very important in the spirit realm. As seen in Isaiah 2:1-4, the world is going *up* to Zion! This *upwards direction in lifestyle* is **not** that which is consistent with the world; it must be different; it must cause the world to turn their heads and take notice of you. This is awesome as all of this began happening since the last days (in the 1ST Century)—and certainly we (in the 21ST Century) qualify to be this type of Church.

It is imperative that we understand that *the spirit realm runs by rank or position*. The Apostle Paul in writing to the church at Ephesus made this very clear:

Ephesians 1:15-2:6 says,

Therefore I also, after I heard of your faith in the Lord Jesus and your love for all the saints, do not cease to give thanks for you, making mention of you in my prayers: that the God of our Lord Jesus Christ, the Father of glory, may give to you the spirit of wisdom and revelation in the knowledge of Him, the eyes of your understanding being enlightened; that you may know what is the hope of His calling, what are the riches of the glory of His inheritance in the saints, and what is the exceeding greatness of His power toward us who believe, according to the working of His mighty power which He worked in Christ when He raised Him from the dead and seated Him at His right hand in the heavenly places, far above all principality and power and might and dominion, and every name that is named, not only in this age but also in that which is to come. And He put all things under His feet, and gave Him to be head over all things to the church, *which is His body, the fullness of Him who fills all in all. And you He made alive, who were dead in trespasses and sins, in which you once walked according to the course of this world, according to the prince of the power of the air, the spirit who now works in the sons of disobedience, among whom also we all once conducted ourselves in the lusts of our flesh, fulfilling the desires of the flesh and of the mind, and were by nature children of wrath, just as the others. But God, who is rich in mercy, because of His great love with which He loved us, even when we were dead in trespasses,* made us alive together with Christ (by grace you have been saved), and raised us up together, and made us sit together in the heavenly places in Christ Jesus."

In describing the Lord's position, the Apostle Paul uses very strong and expressive language—***far above all!*** Jesus is not just above all principalities, powers, might and dominion; He is *at an extreme distance above* them all!

Apostles are mandated to bring the Church into a clear understanding of this fact. They want to see every Believer conformed to the Image of Christ. Apostle Paul's earnest cry for the Saints was that they saw, comprehended and entered into the awesome revelation of "Christ in you the hope of glory." Apostle Paul accentuated that fact when he went on to establish that when Jesus was positioned ***far above all*, we were *raised up together with Him!*** We are positioned in the same place that Jesus is and we must know and realize this.

Let me reemphasize the fact that the spirit realm works by an *internal sense of your position—position is vital.* We just have to know this and be very conscious of the fact, because the devil will try everything possible to negate this fact.

Jesus is *lifted up over every other* name. *He has the highest rank or position.* When we pray "in the name of Jesus" it is *from a position we hold in Him while* we are praying, and not just a religious phrase we are using—not just something we add on to our prayers for power.

In Jesus Name!—It Is A Spiritual Location From Which We Function from—It Is A Lifestyle—It Is An Identity

We cannot function in the spirit realm with condemnation—*we must be confident in our position in Him*—we must know our significance in *Him*! This is the mentality of apostolic people in the *"Zion Church"*.

THE REALITY OF WHAT JESUS ACCOMPLISHED
Ephesians 4:8-10 says,

> *Therefore He says: "When He ascended on high, He led captivity captive, And gave gifts to men." (Now this, "He ascended"—what does it mean but that He also first descended into the lower parts of the earth? He who descended is also the One who ascended far above all the heavens, that He might fill all things.)*

- He descended then He *arose*.
- He went into the deepest depths of hell and then arose.
- Every place the soles of your feet tread is yours.
- *Jesus* has control and authority over every realm from heaven to the lowest part of hell.

We as Born-Again Believers have the same authority because of Jesus—We *sit with Him* in Heavenly places.

For those of you who still have problems with condemnation, hear me—this is the hour for you to *break away* from your past life of condemnation! Remember *He ascended that He might fill all things!* And He has taken us with Him, as we are also seated in heavenly places *in* Christ.

PRINCIPLE TWO—PSALM 48:4-7
The next facet we see of this *"end-time"* Church is the intensity of its warfare as the kings of the earth join forces to seek its destruction: Here is what it says,

> *When the kings joined forces, when they advanced together, they saw [her] and were astounded; they fled in terror. Trembling seized them there, pain like that of a woman in labour. You destroyed them like ships of Tarshish shattered by an* east wind. (NIV)

The East wind was known for its dry, arid nature and it blew in from the wilderness. The Lord will use this wind at times to destroy our comfort zone, as this is what the wilderness was designed to do. Our comfort zone oftentimes stand between us and our destiny. In Acts 27:14 we read of a wind called Euroclydon (translated east wind) that stirred up the waves and caused a tempest! Not every tempest in our lives is caused by the devil as there are times when the Lord will allow trials and tempests in our lives.

THE KINGS OF THE EARTH—THEY ARE ADVERSARIES.

They assemble and advance against the Zion Church. These are not little "6 inch" devils that cause Pastors to divorce their wives and marry their secretaries. NO! These are big devils; they are high-ranking demonic powers and they will seek to dismantle, disjoint, and completely destroy the ZION Church.

THEY SAW IT (the implication here is that they saw and understood what was happening. They saw and heard).

They scrutinized it: they carefully checked out this ZION Church/ STRONGHOLD—this was not a casual glancing; this was intense scrutiny with a microscopic lens. **LOOK AT EPHESIANS 3:8-12** which says,

To me, who am less than the least of all the saints, this grace was given, that I should preach among the Gentiles the unsearchable riches of Christ, and to make all see what is the fellowship of the mystery, which from the beginning of the ages has been hidden in God who created all things through Jesus Christ; to the intent that now the manifold wisdom of God might be made known by the church to the principalities and powers in the heavenly places, *according to the eternal purpose which He accomplished in Christ Jesus our Lord, in whom we have boldness and access with confidence through faith in Him.*

When they saw and heard the Zion Church, they MARVELLED! It is the word ASTONISHED!

They were in CONFUSION and CONSTERNATION!

The kingdom of darkness is in trouble with a ZION CHURCH—The result, THEY FLED IN TERROR (Psalm 48:4-7 NIV)!

This is what a ZION CHURCH does to the enemy. The Church of the Lord Jesus Christ continues to rise strong in the earth.

This is why every local church needs to have the apostolic dimension in it. Part of the apostolic calling and mantle is the ability to dismantle demonic thrones and powers. The apostolic anointing can penetrate and dismantle inaccurate mindsets and thought patterns established by these "demonic kings of the earth". The Apostle Paul effectively describes this apostolic dimension in 2 Corinthians 10:4-6 when he said:

For the weapons of our warfare are not carnal but mighty in God for pulling down strongholds, casting down arguments and every high thing that exalts itself against the knowledge of God, bringing every thought into captivity to the obedience of Christ, and being ready to punish all disobedience when your obedience is fulfilled.

Psalm 48:8 says,

As we have heard, So we have seen *In the city of the LORD of hosts, In the city of our God: God will establish it forever.* Selah"

PRINCIPLE THREE—AS WE HAVE HEARD SO HAVE WE SEEN
There has been too much hearing and no seeing. The ZION Church is the place where you can SEE the Lord and not a charismatic man or personality, where there is vision that is centred in the Lord.

It Is A Place Where The Walk Matches The Talk!

It is an apostolic Church that can decode and bring to reality the mysteries of the Lord as the Apostle Peter did on the Day of Pentecost in Acts 2:14-16 which says,

But Peter, standing up with the eleven, raised his voice and said to them, "Men of Judea and all who dwell in Jerusalem, let this be known to you, and heed my words. For these are not drunk, as you suppose, since it is only the third hour of the day. But this is what was spoken by the prophet Joel:"

Here Apostle Peter received revelation as to what was occurring when the Holy Spirit arrived. Others saw men drunk with wine, but he rightly decoded the event—"these men are not drunk. No! These men are filled with the Holy Spirit as spoken by the Prophet Joel some 800 years before."

What you have heard, we now bring into manifestation, Apostle Peter was rightly and boldly declaring things and we need to do the same! The Fortress Church allows the Word to BECOME flesh and live through the Saints.

That's why we have to hate hypocrisy and double-mindedness. Our souls have to hate hesitancy—we must leave behind the lame and the blind.

If we are not careful the Lord will have to check some of us into the Inn, like He did Moses in Exodus 4:24-26 KJV, which says,

> *And it came to pass by the way in the inn, that the LORD met him, and sought to kill him. Then Zipporah took a sharp stone, and cut off the foreskin of her son, and cast it at his feet, and said, Surely a bloody husband art thou to me. So he let him go: then she said, A bloody husband thou art, because of the circumcision.*

Moses just received the longest prophecy in the Bible (see Exodus chapters 3-4). However, he forgot to circumcise his son. Regardless of how important you may think of what God has given you to do, you cannot be hesitant when it comes to your family duties. God MUST have complete access to our lives.

Psalm 48:9-11 says,

> *Within your temple, O God, we meditate on your unfailing love. Like your name, O God, your praise reaches to the ends of the earth; your right hand is filled with righteousness.* Mount Zion rejoices, the villages of Judah are glad because of your judgements. (NIV)

PRINCIPLE FOUR—MATURE JOY

This type of joy is produced as a result of God's judgement.

We have to progress beyond the initial joy of Salvation. In the ZION CHURCH we will come to a place of Mature Joy: There is Joy because of God's Judgement!

Judgement—this is not speaking about God's punishment. It is referring to the Lord's justice or decision. It is God becoming the Sovereign Lord over our lives.

This Mature Joy is produced when we walk accurately in God. When we allow our steps to be ordered and ordained by Him.

It is maturity when we can submit to the Hand and Process of Almighty God—It is immaturity when we cannot seem to submit as we are brought under the Mighty Hand of God or brought under the scrutiny of God.

Psalm 48:12-13 says,

Walk about Zion, go around her, count her towers, consider well her ramparts, view her citadels, that you may tell of them to the next generation. (NIV)

PRINCIPLE FIVE—GENERATIONAL BLESSINGS

The *"Zion Church"* is an exemplar, model or prototype Church. We must declare that it is possible to build a Strong Church. A Church that reclaims its *Generational Power*, a Church that can last through the generations, with a sense of purpose and direction.

The *"Zion Church"* seeks to destroy the spirit that causes the next generation to be lost. That happened under Joshua and so many others, throughout the history of the Church.

Judges 2:8-12 says,

Now Joshua the son of Nun, the servant of the LORD, died when he was one hundred and ten years old. And they buried him within the border of his inheritance at Timnath Heres, in the mountains of Ephraim, on the north side of Mount Gaash. When all that generation had been gathered to their fathers, another generation arose after them who did not know the LORD nor the work which He had done for Israel. Then the children of Israel did evil in the sight of the LORD, and served the Baals; and they forsook the LORD God of their fathers, who had brought them out of the land of Egypt; and they followed other gods from among the gods of the people who were all around them, and they bowed down to them; and they provoked the LORD to anger.

From that time the Lord allowed Judges to lead the people, when His true desire was to have kings (a type of the apostolic) over them. And when the Judge followed the Lord, they did what was right and when the Judge chose to do his own thing, the things of the Lord were forsaken as there was no internal self-government formed in the people.

The *"Zion Church"* will be a true *"Fathering"* Church with an Elijah spirit, where the hearts of the fathers have truly been turned to the children and the heart of the children turned to their fathers, resulting in true *"Generational Blessings"*.

Another dimension of this *"Zion Church"* is the grace anointing from the Lord needed to bring in the Harvest. This type of Church was also spoken of in the book of Isaiah: Isaiah 2:1-4 says,

> *The word that Isaiah the son of Amoz saw concerning Judah and Jerusalem.* Now it shall come to pass in the latter days That the mountain of the LORD's house Shall be established on the top of the mountains, And shall be exalted above the hills; And all nations shall flow to it. *Many people shall come and say,* "Come, and let us go up to the mountain of the LORD, *To the house of the God of Jacob; He will teach us His ways, And we shall walk in His paths."* For out of Zion shall go forth the law, *And the word of the LORD from Jerusalem. He shall judge between the nations, And rebuke many people;* They shall beat their swords into ploughshares, And their spears into pruning hooks; *Nation shall not lift up sword against nation, Neither shall they learn war anymore.*

This is so awesome! The Prophet Isaiah is given this panoramic view of the Church as it was launched in the "last days", and it truly was powerfully prophetic to be viewing the future in his time!

We would all agree that Isaiah is indeed speaking about the Church, the Lord's House, Zion if you will, of that there should be no doubt. This Church was born in the last days of Israel's reign and continues to this very day.

Just as we touched on earlier, this Church will be in an elevated position, her status of being *"seated in heavenly places in Christ Jesus"* will be further accentuated in our day.

Contrary to some popular opinions, this Church that began in the 1ST Century and is still alive today will continue to see the nations coming to her for guidance. This is already occurring in some quarters as leaders of nations seek out the counsel of godly men. This Church is described as established and exalted. This is the mandate upon the *"Five-Fold"* ministry, to bring the Church of the Living God to a place of ordained strength and maturity. I love how the Apostle Paul declares it in the following passage: Romans 16:25-27 says,

Now to Him who is able to establish you according to my gospel and the preaching of Jesus Christ, according to the revelation of the mystery kept secret since the world began but now has been made manifest, and by the prophetic Scriptures has been made known to all nations, according to the commandment of the everlasting God, *for obedience to the faith - to God, alone wise, be glory through Jesus Christ forever. Amen.*

FOR OUT OF ZION SHALL GO FORTH THE LAW

The Prophet goes on to declare that the law will proceed out of **Zion**. The law here is not referring to legalism but instead it is referring to lifestyle principles. This *"Zion Church"* will be a place where the Saints will be walking in *"Lifestyle Christianity"*, not Sunday morning theatrics. They will demonstrate the quality of life for which, our Lord Jesus Christ purchased with His Blood.

I like what the Apostle Paul said to the church at Philippi in Philippians 2:12-15, which says,

Therefore, my beloved, as you have always obeyed, not as in my presence only, but now much more in my absence, work out your own salvation with fear and trembling; for it is God who works in you both to will and to do for His good pleasure. Do all things without complaining and disputing, that you may become blameless and harmless, children of God without fault in the midst of a crooked and perverse generation, among whom you shine as lights in the world.

We talk about God and how much we love Him and how good He is, but we often live like atheists—murmuring and complaining all the time. We are not to live this way. Believers in a true "Zion Church" do not live this way. They understand that this is the lifestyle of a true Believer, one who does not compromise their walk among the unsaved in this world.

So many fall apart in the midst of trials and the world says; "where's their God?"

The Apostle Paul was a great example of this level of lifestyle. After all he and Apostle Silas were cast in the inner prison of a Philippians' jail where they experienced a tremendous testimony. Here is an account of that incident:

Acts 16:16-34 says,

Now it happened, as we went to prayer, that a certain slave girl possessed with a spirit of divination met us, who brought her masters much profit by fortune-telling. This girl followed Paul and us, and cried out, saying, "These men are the servants of the Most High God, who proclaim to us the way of salvation." And this she did for many days. But Paul, greatly annoyed, turned and said to the spirit, "I command you in the name of Jesus Christ to come out of her." And he came out that very hour. But when her masters saw that their hope of profit was gone, they seized Paul and Silas and dragged them into the marketplace to the authorities. And they brought them to the magistrates, and said, "These men, being Jews, exceedingly trouble our city; and they teach customs which are not lawful for us, being Romans, to receive or observe." Then the multitude rose up together against them; and the magistrates tore off their clothes and commanded them to be beaten with rods. And when they had laid many stripes on them, they threw them into prison, commanding the jailer to keep them securely. Having received such a charge, he put them into the inner prison and fastened their feet in the stocks. But at midnight Paul and Silas were praying and singing hymns to God, and the prisoners were listening to them. *Suddenly there was a great earthquake, so that the foundations of the prison were shaken; and immediately all the doors were opened and everyone's chains were loosed. And the keeper of the prison, awaking from sleep and seeing the prison doors open, supposing the prisoners had fled, drew his sword and was about to kill himself. But Paul called with a loud voice, saying, "Do yourself no harm, for we are all here." Then he called for a light, ran in, and fell down trembling before Paul and Silas. And he brought them out and said, "Sirs, what must I do to be saved?" So they said, "Believe on the Lord Jesus Christ, and you will be saved, you and your household." Then they spoke the word of the Lord to him and to all who were in his house. And he took them the same hour of the night and washed their stripes. And immediately he and all his family were baptized. Now when he had brought them into his house, he set food before them; and he rejoiced, having believed in God with all his household."*

We know that they began praying and a certain slave girl with a spirit of divination (who incidentally raked in a tidy sum of wealth for her masters) followed them making some bold proclamations over them. When that spirit began to aggravate Apostle Paul he rebuked the girl and cast that spirit out of her. Because she was a major source of revenue to her city, Paul's castigation did not go over so well and Apostles Paul and Silas were stripped of all clothing and severely beaten before being thrown into the prison. Here are a few questions that we could ask!

- What if they would have been murmuring and complaining and griping about their situation?
- What if Silas would have said, "Paul, you sure like to act the big shot! You had to show off and cast the demon out of that girl. Now look at the trouble we're in. Why couldn't you just leave that demon possessed girl alone?" And then Paul fired back, "Listen Silas, why didn't you tell them we're Roman citizens and they wouldn't have beaten us. But, no, you had to keep your mouth shut."

Tell me if that had been going on between Paul and Silas do you think the jailor would have asked, "What must I do to be saved?" I doubt it! He probably would have said, "What must I do to stay away from this Christianity thing?"

Fellow Saints, our testimony is important, so very important. God uses our lives to influence others. We live in a fallen world, and by circumstance, a fallen world is not easy to live and navigate in for the Believer, but we are not to complain.

However, there is something of tremendous note that occurs in this "*Zion Church*"... a command goes forth for them to *beat their swords into ploughshares, And their spears into pruning hooks*. This is powerful for two reasons as it implies the following:

Firstly, in order for the Church to get to the place of being established on top of the mountain, she had to war her way to it. She arrived at the top of the mountain with sword and spear in hand. This is why the Church today must have Apostles within her if we are to arrive at this predetermined destination of ruling among the nations. Apostles are being released by the Lord in this hour, to sharpen us in understanding the Will and Purpose of the Lord. Knowledge is power, which is why Daniel declared: Daniel 11:32-33 says,

> *Those who do wickedly against the covenant he shall corrupt with flattery;* but the people who know their God shall be strong, and carry out great exploits. And those of the people who understand shall instruct many...

Remember, we the Saints, are the Lord's Battle Axes. We are the ones He uses in accomplishing His will. As we are sharpened in our understanding of Him and His perfect will, we can then execute His written judgements. There is a massive warfare for the minds of men. The mind is the biggest and greatest battleground, for the Word of God declares "For *as he thinks* in his heart, *so is he.*" Proverbs 23:7 (Emphasis added). The Apostle Paul also describes it this way: 2 Corinthians 10:4-6 says,

> For the weapons of our warfare *are not carnal but mighty in God for pulling down strongholds,* casting down arguments and every high thing that exalts itself against the knowledge of God, bringing every thought into captivity to the obedience of Christ, *and being ready to punish all disobedience when your obedience is fulfilled.*

He clearly shows us that the battle is in the thought realm. Hence, part of the mandate given to Apostles is the ability and grace to destroy wrong mindsets, concepts and principles that have been established in the minds of the Saints, and replace them with correct ones.

Secondly, as this continues to be accomplished, we are going to see one of the largest harvests of souls the world has ever seen. The command goes forth for the Saints to *beat their swords into ploughshares, And their spears into pruning hooks.* The Saints' weapons of warfare have now returned to farming implements, which is being used to accomplish the greatest harvest of the ages.

Chapter Seven
Indeed We Have Come To Mt. Zion

THE BOOK OF HEBREWS WAS WRITTEN TO A GROUP OF SUFFERING, PERSECUTED Jewish Believers who because of the persecution were tempted to turn away from Christianity and return to Judaism. The writer warned them that to do so would put them in the category of Esau who sacrificed his birthright for a bowl of stew. If they turned away from Christ, they too would be as Esau and they would deeply regret it.

Throughout this epistle the writer has contrasted the Old Covenant with the New Covenant time and time again within the body of the text, in order to show the superiority of the New Covenant and our Lord's High Priesthood. The writer has also emphasized that the greater privilege of the New Covenant also brought a greater responsibility for the Believers in Jesus Christ.

The writer of Hebrews made a very powerful statement to the 1ST Century Saints as the New Covenant was being established when he penned the following in Hebrews 12:18-29, which says,

For you have not come to the mountain that may be touched and that burned with fire, and to blackness and darkness and tempest, and the sound of a trumpet and the voice of words, so that those who heard it begged that the word should not be spoken to them anymore. (For they could not endure what was commanded: "And if so much as a beast touches the mountain, it shall be stoned or shot with an arrow." And so terrifying was the sight that Moses said, "I am exceedingly afraid and trembling.") But you have come to Mount Zion and to the city of the living God, the heavenly Jerusalem, to an innumerable company of angels, to the general assembly and church of the firstborn who are registered in heaven, to God the Judge of all, to the spirits of just men made perfect, to Jesus the Mediator of the new covenant, and to the blood of sprinkling that speaks better things than that of Abel. See that you do not refuse Him who speaks. For if they did not escape who refused Him who spoke on earth, much more shall we not escape if we turn away from Him who speaks from heaven, whose voice then shook the earth; but now He has promised, saying, "Yet once more I shake not only the earth, but also heaven." Now this, "Yet once more," indicates the removal of those things that are being shaken, as of things that are made, that the things which cannot be shaken may remain. Therefore, since we are receiving a kingdom which cannot be shaken, let us have grace, by which we may serve God acceptably with reverence and godly fear. For our God is a consuming fire.

What was the purpose of these contrasts? It was to provide a basis of warning to those who were considering going back to the Old Covenant and its rituals. Just as Peter who was disillusioned about his calling as one of the 12 when Jesus was crucified, and returned to fishing, many of the new converts vacillated about their faith. The writer of Hebrews was warning them by means of contrast in order to have them truly consider their choices.

This final warning has two parts:

1. Verses 18-24 contrasts the Old Covenant with the New Covenant showing the superior privileges of the New Covenant, and therefore, the greater responsibility we have under it.
2. Verses 25-29 show the necessity to heed the Voice of the God of that Covenant. If they were punished in the Old Covenant for refusing to listen to Him who spoke from Sinai, **how much more severe** will be the punishment that comes upon those who refuse to listen to Him who speaks from Mt. Zion.

Verses 18-21 describe the events, which took place on Mt. Sinai when the 10 commandments were given to Moses, and the Mosaic covenant was enacted. This description of the terrors of Sinai is drawn from Exodus 19. Let's look at it together:

Exodus 19:7-12 says,

So Moses came and called for the elders of the people, and laid before them all these words, which the LORD commanded him. Then all the people answered together and said, "All that the LORD has spoken we will do." So Moses brought back the words of the people to the LORD. And the LORD said to Moses, "Behold, I come to you in the thick cloud, that the people may hear when I speak with you, and believe you forever." So Moses told the words of the people to the LORD. ¹⁰ Then the LORD said to Moses, "Go to the people and consecrate them today and tomorrow, and let them wash their clothes. ¹¹ And let them be ready for the third day. For on the third day the LORD will come down upon Mount Sinai in the sight of all the people. ¹² You shall set bounds for the people all around, saying, 'Take heed to yourselves that you do not go up to the mountain or touch its base. Whoever touches the mountain shall surely be put to death."

Notice in verse 12 the contrast to what we've been seeing in Hebrews. God's Presence is restricted here, but In the New Covenant we have free access to God:

Hebrews 4:14-16 says,

Seeing then that we have a great High Priest who has passed through the heavens, Jesus the Son of God, let us hold fast our confession. For we do not have a High Priest who cannot sympathize with our weaknesses, but was in all points tempted as we are, yet without sin. Let us therefore come boldly to the throne of grace, that we may obtain mercy and find grace to help in time of need.

Here we are told not to stay away but to come **boldly** to the Throne of Grace. Apostle Paul confirms this in Romans:

Romans 5:1-2 says,

Therefore, having been justified by faith, we have peace with God through our Lord Jesus Christ, through whom also we have access by faith into this grace in which we stand, and rejoice in hope of the glory of God.

As we see, we have peace and access to God. And further, the Apostle John wrote to us in the book of Revelation:

Revelation 21:1-3 says,

Now I saw a new heaven and a new earth, for the first heaven and the first earth had passed away. Also there was no more sea. Then I, John, saw the holy city, New Jerusalem, coming down out of heaven from God, prepared as a bride adorned for her husband. And I heard a loud voice from heaven saying, "Behold, the tabernacle of God is with men, and He will dwell with them, and they shall be His people. God Himself will be with them and be their God.

In the Old Covenant, Exodus 19:12 holds dire consequences for him who comes near, "whoever touches the mountain shall surely be put to death." Why? Because God is Holy while man is sinful. It was so extreme that God wanted man to be aware of the separation that sin has caused.

They weren't even allowed to touch that which touched the mountain. They had to kill it from a distance. Exodus 19:13 "'Not a hand shall touch him, but he shall surely be stoned or shot with an arrow; whether man or beast, he shall not live." Our New Covenant has done away with all of this ritual and warnings, as God is not warning men to step back but rather He is near as He dwells with us!

The Old Covenant people because of their sin were unable to draw near to God's Presence. What a contrast we have here between this and Zion.

Hebrews 12:18-21 says,

For you have not come to the mountain that may be touched and that burned with fire, and to blackness and darkness and tempest, and the sound of a trumpet and the voice of words, so that those who heard it begged that the word should not be spoken to them

*anymore. (For they could not endure what was commanded: "And if
so much as a beast touches the mountain, it shall be stoned or shot
with an arrow." And so terrifying was the sight that Moses said, "I
am exceedingly afraid and trembling.)*

Put yourself in the sandals of an Israelite standing thunderstruck and
in awe at the foot of that mountain. You have probably seen the power of
a severe thunderstorm in all of its power and disruption: imagine what
being near the mountain was like for the Israelite.

In verse 21 Moses said, *"I exceedingly fear and quake."* Moses was the
leader of the people. He was known as one who had an especially close
relationship with God: (see Exodus 33:11)

The writer of Hebrews was saying, "People, don't turn back to that
system, to do so is to come under God's judgement."

I doubt very seriously that any of you are being tempted to turn back
to the Mosaic covenant. But it's important that we understand that the
principle still applies. I'm sure that there are some of you who are or
have been tempted to turn away from your Christian testimony in order
to escape the persecution that comes from it.

The threat of apostasy that they were facing is still very real today. In
fact, I believe that *many* Believers live in a state of apostasy and are squan-
dering away their rewards. I know many people who, because of the trials
of life, have become bitter at God and left the Church. This warning against
apostasy is very relevant to us today, and it is a sin we must guard against.

Most Believers don't understand that we live in a different age than
Apostle Paul did. Apostle Paul lived in what the Bible calls the "last
days"—they were the last days of the Old Covenant. Those "last days"
began at Pentecost and ended at AD 70 when the Jewish temple was completely destroyed. We now live in what the Bible calls "the age to come",
which is the New Covenant age. The forty-year period, from Pentecost
to Holocaust (the time of the destruction of the Temple and slaughter of
many Jews), was a time of *transition* from the Old Covenant to the New
Covenant. In this transition period, the New Covenant had been inaugu-
rated but not consummated. It was a time of "already but not yet."

Here is another thought that we must consider: The heavenly
Jerusalem is the New Covenant and can be clearly seen in: Galatians 4:21-
31 says,

Tell me, you who desire to be under the law, do you not hear the law? For it is written that Abraham had two sons: the one by a bondwoman, the other by a freewoman. But he who was of the bondwoman was born according to the flesh, and he of the freewoman through promise, which things are symbolic. For these are the two covenants: the one from Mount Sinai which gives birth to bondage, which is Hagar; for this Hagar is Mount Sinai in Arabia, and corresponds to Jerusalem which now is, and is in bondage with her children; *but the* Jerusalem above is free, which is the mother of us all. *For it is written: "Rejoice, O barren, You who do not bear! Break forth and shout, You who are not in labor! For the desolate has many more children Than she who has a husband." Now we, brethren, as Isaac was, are children of promise. But, as he who was born according to the flesh then persecuted him who was born according to the Spirit,* even so it is now *[during the transition period in which this writing was done]. Nevertheless what does the Scripture say? "Cast out the bondwoman and her son, for the son of the bondwoman shall not be heir with the son of the freewoman." So then, brethren, we are not children of the bondwoman but of the free.*

In this allegory, we have two women who are also said to be two cities, and they derive their origin from TWO COVENANTS, giving birth to two kinds of children:

The first is Hagar, answering to **physical Jerusalem**, unto who was born a nation after the flesh.

The second is **Sarah, answering to New Jerusalem**, unto who was born a nation after the Spirit.

These two nations, or "Israelis", are the theme of Old Testament prophecy, the gospels, the epistles, and finally the Revelation message.

Just as Hagar and her son (Old Covenant system and people) coexisted for some time with Sarah and her son (New Covenant system and people), so also both Covenant systems coexisted for a time. However, the bondwoman and her son were eventually cast out, just as the Old Covenant system would be cast out when God finished His redemptive work in the AD 70 destruction of Jerusalem.

We, as 21ST Century Believers, are NOT receiving a Kingdom; the Kingdom arrived in its fullness in AD 70 with the destruction of Jerusalem. We live in this spiritual, eternal Kingdom of God that will never be shaken: Daniel 2:44 says,

And in the days of these kings the God of heaven will set up a kingdom which shall never be destroyed; and the kingdom shall not be left to other people; it shall break in pieces and consume all these kingdoms, and it shall stand forever.

But to the First Century Saints, the Kingdom had not arrived in its fullness, so, our author exhorts his readers, *"...let us have grace".* What they needed on the way to receiving this Kingdom was Grace. That Grace, we have learned was, and still is available through our High Priest, Jesus Christ at the throne of Grace.

He goes on to say, ***"...by which we may serve God acceptably with reverence and godly fear"***. God's Grace is always provided for enablement in serving God. Since this Kingdom is eternal, we should devote our lives to serving in it. And that this service should be with ***"reverence and godly fear"*** which are appropriate in light of all that has been said about our relationship to God.

This is another reminder that the God of Sinai is the same God of Zion. He was warning them of the dreadful consequences of abandoning their faith in God. Apostasy, as they had already been told, can only mean one thing: *"a certain fearful expectation of judgment, and fiery indignation which will devour the adversaries"* (Hebrews 10:27).

Believers, our salvation is secure, Jesus has paid our sin debt, and He has given us His righteousness. But this is not a license to sin: we are responsible for how we live, and if we fail to hear Him who speaks from Heaven, we will be disciplined. God will discipline us here and now, and we will lose our rewards for all eternity.

In the final chapter of this book I would like for us to look at how we should live in the Kingdom Age. Let us now take that journey.

CHAPTER EIGHT
LIVING IN THE KINGDOM AGE

THE "NEW AGE" HAS ALREADY DAWNED, AND THE CHURCH IS LIVING IN THAT AGE.

When I speak of this "New Age" I am referring to the "New Covenant Age"... After all when the Scriptures were written they were written under the "Old Age" or "Old Covenant System" and during the time of transition between the Old and the New Covenants...

Hear me: The miracle of Pentecost that took place almost 2000 years ago was proof that the "end-times" had already begun, for the outpouring of the Spirit spoken of by Joel had taken place, and continue to this very day...

Joel 2:28-32 says,

And it shall come to pass afterward That I will pour out My Spirit on all flesh; Your sons and your daughters shall prophesy, Your old men shall dream dreams, Your young men shall see visions. And also on My menservants and on My maidservants I will pour out My Spirit in those days. And I will show wonders in the heavens and in the earth: Blood and fire and pillars of smoke. The sun shall be turned into darkness, And the moon into blood, Before the coming of the great and awesome day of the LORD. And it shall come to pass That whoever calls on the name of the LORD Shall be saved. For in Mount Zion and in Jerusalem there shall be deliverance, As the LORD has said, Among the remnant whom the LORD calls.

Acts 2:15-21 says,

For these are not drunk, as you suppose, since it is only the third hour of the day. But this is what was spoken by the prophet Joel: 'And it shall come to pass in the last days, says God, That I will pour out of My Spirit on all flesh; Your sons and your daughters shall prophesy, Your young men shall see visions, Your old men shall dream dreams. And on My menservants and on My maidservants I will pour out My Spirit in those days; And they shall prophesy. I will show wonders in heaven above And signs in the earth beneath: Blood and fire and vapor of smoke. The sun shall be turned into darkness, And the moon into blood, Before the coming of the great and awesome day of the LORD. And it shall come to pass That whoever calls on the name of the LORD Shall be saved.'

The Believer back then had been delivered out of "this present evil age" (Galatians 1:4), had tasted the powers of the Age to come (Hebrews 6:5), and has transferred his citizenship to that age (Philippians 3:20). The New Testament Church saw itself as the people of that Kingdom, the "eschatological community" which was living already in that Age to come.

The leadership of the Church must have a revelation of the Kingdom of God and of the restoration of Zion. Leaders must be able to impart this revelation into Believers in order for them to live and enjoy the benefits of this Age.

Israel looked for the Kingdom Age and received hope from their Prophets. They lived under the dominion of the Assyrians, Babylonians, Persians, Greeks, and Romans. They looked forward to the day of the Messiah and the Messianic Age. Jesus came proclaiming that that Age had arrived.

The Kingdom Age was further initiated on the day of Pentecost. The outpouring of the Holy Spirit signalled the beginning of the age of blessing upon all flesh. The Kingdom Age was to be a Prophetic Age with dreams, visions, signs and wonders. It would also be an age of judgment upon those who resisted the Kingdom (see Psalms chapter 2, Acts 4:23-27).

The apostolic anointing is unique to this Age. The prophetic anointing is joined to the apostolic to operate as foundational anointings during this Age. These anointings help prepare God's people to live and minister during this Age. The local church is a Kingdom embassy. Apostles and apostolic people are Kingdom ambassadors and emissaries. They operate in the authority and power of the King of the Kingdom. They preach the message of the Kingdom (the Gospel).

The apostolic anointing prepares people to live and operate in this Kingdom Age through preaching, teaching, impartation, activation, and revelation. Apostles preach and demonstrate the power of the Kingdom (see Matthew chapter 10).

The Kingdom Age is an age of knowledge (see Isaiah 2:2-3, Romans 15:14).

The Kingdom Age is an age of worship (see Psalms 22:27-28), Jesus sings in the midst of the Church during the Messianic Age (see Psalms 22:22, Hebrews 2:19).

Jesus is the chief singer and chief musician (50 of the Psalms begin with the heading "To the chief musician"). The LORD sings over us (see Zephaniah 3:16).

The Messianic Age is an age of new songs (see Psalms 40:3, Psalms 96:1, Psalms 98:1).

True worship always has been and always will be prophetic, alive with the thoughts and voice of God. Revelation 19:10 connects worship and prophecy. Here it was it says,

> *And I fell at his feet to worship him. But he said to me, "See that you do not do that! I am your fellow servant, and of your brethren who have the testimony of Jesus. Worship God! For the testimony of Jesus is the spirit of prophecy."*

The Baptism of the Holy Spirit prepares every Believer to participate in prophetic worship during this Kingdom Age. We cannot underestimate the power of the prophetic song. The following verse suggests that the song is such that it will be seen, and those who see it will be in awe of the Lord and will put their trust in Him: Psalms 40:3 says,

> *He has put a new song in my mouth—Praise to our God; Many will see it and fear, And will trust in the LORD.*

- The Kingdom Age in which we live is an age of singing and shouting (see Isaiah 12:6, Zephaniah 3:14-15, Zechariah 9:9).
- The Kingdom Age in which we live is an age of Salvation (see Isaiah 52:10, Acts 2:21).
- The Kingdom Age in which we live is an age of deliverance (see Obadiah 17,21, Colossians 1:13).
- The Kingdom Age in which we live is an age of glory (see Habakkuk 2:14, Corinthians 3:11).
- The Kingdom Age in which we live is an age of the Holy Spirit (see Joel 2, Ezekiel 36:25-27, Acts 2).
- This is a Prophetic Age (see Joel 2, Acts 2).
- This is an Apostolic Age (se Luke 11:49).
- This is an age of restoration (Zion and the tabernacle of David) (see Amos 9:11-13, 1 Chronicles 25, Acts 15:15-17).
- This is an age of prophetic fulfillment (see Mark 1:15).
- This is an age of prayer and intercession (see Isaiah 56:7, 62:6-7).
- This is an age of the nations (see Psalms 117, Romans 15:9-12).
- This is an age of tribulation (see John 16:33, Revelation 7:14).
- This Kingdom Age is an age of judgment (see Joel 3:2, Revelation 16:7),
- This Kingdom Age is an age of favour and mercy (see Psalms chapter 102, Romans 15:9).
- This Kingdom Age is an age of prosperity and blessing (see Ezekiel 34:26, Ephesians 1:3).

SOME CHARACTERISTICS OF THE HIGH CALLING, OF ZION THE PEOPLE

- They are kings, seated and established (Psalms 2:6). They show forth all His praise (Psalms 9:14) and are called to aid and strengthen the nations (Psalms 20:2).
- The people of Zion are safe and secure in Christ, (Psalms 48:112-113) and are the light of the world, radiating the image of God (Psalms 50:2).
- The people of God move forward, growing in grace from strength to strength (see Psalms 84:7), dwell in peace and prosperity (Psalms 76:2), and bring salvation, joy, and gladness (Psalms 53:6).
- The people of Zion constitute a Kingdom that cannot be shaken or moved (Psalms 125:1) and hated by the wicked (Psalms 129:5).

- The people of Zion are the habitation (resting-place) of God Psalms 132:13-14) and reign with God (Psalms 146:10) as they are ever joyful in their King (Psalms 149:2)

Our metamorphosis, our maturing in grace is a steady ascent into the hill of the Lord... the only message that will transform people and change the world is the Gospel of the Kingdom, the message of Zion! Zion is the high place of the Kingdom, the destiny of the most high Saints of the most holy place (see Daniel 7:19-27).

Zion is being restored (see Isaiah 64:10, 65:18-19). Isaiah chapters 60 and 61 prophesies the glory of restored Zion.

Comfort and joy are the characteristics of restored Zion (see Isaiah 51:3, 11).

Zion is awakening (see Isaiah chapter 52). Apostles and Prophets are a part of this awakening.

The trumpet is being blown in Zion (see Joel 2:1).

Zion is the prophetic and poetic name of the worshipping people, or "nation" that will arise in the "*last days*". This nation will consist of a great company of worshippers who display God's splendour and defeat His enemies. New prophetic sounds and culture will be found in the midst of Zion (see Isaiah 42:10). Every nation has been called to Zion—to be birthed in worship, dwell in His courts and run after His Presence forever. Singers and players of instruments dwell in Zion (see Psalms 87:7).

- The nations are asking the way to Zion (see Jeremiah 50:5).
- The Lord appears in His glory after Zion is built up (see Psalms 102:16).
- Zion is a chosen place. It is God's dwelling place forever (see Psalms 132:13).
- Zion is the place of God's Glory and Presence. The good news to Zion is "thy God reigneth" (Isaiah 52:7 KJV).
- Zion is a high place of abundance (see Jeremiah 31:6, 12-14).
- Zion is a place of victory and judgment. It is the place of the overcoming remnant (see Revelation 14).
- The Kingdom and Zion are inseparable.

David established Zion as his place of rule and worship. David established prophetic worship in Zion. The "tent" of David was the place of the Ark (Presence of God) and prophetic families (Asaph, Heman, and Jeduthun, see 1 Chronicles chapter 25). The Church should be a prophetic family.

Prophetic families (local churches) will worship prophetically in Zion (new songs, spontaneous songs, spiritual songs).

- Are we building "Zion" churches?
- Are we preaching the Gospel of the Kingdom?
- Are we preaching and releasing the Kingdom?
- Do our people understand who they are?
- Are they responding to the high calling to Zion?
- Are we seeing Zion restored in every locality?

Please understand that, we, the Church have come to and are now a part of Mt. Zion the city of the great King.

It is my prayer that the revelation contained within the pages of this book would become a source of blessing and encouragement to you and yours. May you progress deep into the plan and purpose of the Lord Jesus Christ. And may your understanding of the significance of Mount Zion open up new vistas of truth and revelation for you! Be blessed!

OTHER TITLES
BY MICHAEL SCANTLEBURY

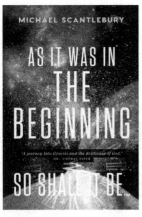

AS IT WAS IN THE BEGINNING SO SHALL IT BE...

Have you ever wondered about life and all of its intricacies? Why are we here on planet earth? What is out there in deep dark space? Who created it all in its majesty and wonder with the brilliancy of everything that surrounds us?

Since time began, man has tried to explain things regarding the known world. One forward thinker put forth a theory that the world was flat. That was refuted by more research. Study and research and pondering some more have revealed some truth about our world but not all the questions are yet answered.

While many of us as Christians enjoy documentaries on the pondering of the many ways we may have "gotten here" beginning with the theory of alien transports dropping us off, to the idea of a cosmic slime pit which one day came to life, so truly the only authority we have as born-again followers of Jesus Christ is the book of Genesis, the very first book of the Holy Scriptures, which simply states: "In the beginning God created the heavens and the earth." Genesis 1:1

We will broach the answers to these and other questions only God's inspired word, the Holy Bible will answer the many questions at hand.

We will begin our journey into the heart and mind of this incredible Creator to learn the reason and purpose for our existence. And as we take that incredible journey, we would seek to come to terms with the revealed, eventual outcome of our existence and life upon planet earth.

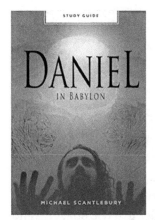

STUDY GUIDE – DANIEL IN BABYLON

This is an exciting study into the present truth lifestyle illustrated through the lives of Daniel and his friends. Whether you'll be meeting with others in a group or going through this book on your own, you've made an excellent decision by choosing to read **DANIEL in Babylon** and studying it in-depth with this guide.

This is a seminal study with strong Apostolic messaging, yet its flowing style allows for easy assimilation of biblical truths, and provides accurate insights for the cerebral believer, who like Daniel and his companions, are usually the target of the world system. In this book various methodologies are outlined through which, spiritual Babylon seeks to entice the brightest and best of every Godly generation, to acculturize, rob of spiritual identity and manipulate to promote world kingdom end.

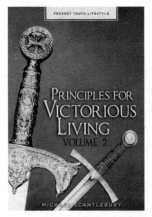

PRINCIPLES FOR VICTORIOUS LIVING VOLUME II

The initial purpose of the five-fold ministry is for the perfecting or maturing of the Saints, which leads to its next intention, which is the real work of the ministry of Jesus Christ, reconciling the world back to the Father. This book lends itself to help in the maturing of the Saints. It adds insight and strategies that help in achieving exponential personal growth preparing one for the real work of the ministry. This is a volume of information and revelation needed in such a time as this, when maturity and focus are the needed key components that bring us an overcoming victory in this realm and advance the Kingdom of God.

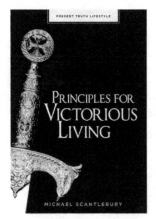

PRINCIPLES FOR VICTORIOUS LIVING VOL I

The information contained herein is well balanced with a spiritual maturity that keenly stems from wisdom and revelation in the knowledge of Christ. This is the anointing of an Apostle, and the truths that our brother shares will certainly cause you to excel in the Kingdom of God long before this life is over when later we enter the eternals. There's so much to experience today in this life, and Michael extracts so much from the Word of God to facilitate that. His insight of revelation and ability to interpret and articulate what his spirit receives from the Lord are powerful.

PRESENT TRUTH LIFESTYLE – DANIEL IN BABYLON

This is a seminal study with strong Apostolic messaging, yet its flowing style allows for easy assimilation of biblical truths, and provides accurate insights for the cerebral believer, who like Daniel and his companions, are usually the target of the world system. In this book various methodologies are outlined through which, spiritual Babylon seeks to entice the brightest and best of every Godly generation, to acculturize, rob of spiritual identity and manipulate to promote world kingdom end.

But thanks be to God, there is still a generation in the earth spiritually alert enough to operate within the world system, yet deploy their talents and giftings to bring honour and glory to God. Those with the Daniel mindset will decode dreams and visions and interpret judgements written on the kingdoms of this world in this season.

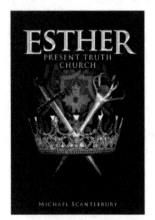

ESTHER PRESENT TRUTH CHURCH

In a season where the Church co-exists harmoniously with truth and error, this book provides us with a precision tool and well-calibrated instrument of change that is able to fine-tune the global Body of Christ.

The Book of Esther is rich with revelation that is still valid and applicable for the day in which we live. Hidden within its pages is a powerful "present truth" message. The lives of the people involved and the conditions that are seen have spiritual parallels for the Church. Our destiny as the Body of Christ is revealed. The preparations and conditions we must attain to are all similar.

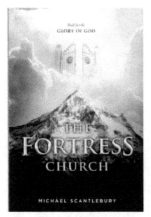

THE FORTRESS CHURCH

According to Webster's English Dictionary "fortress" is defined as: a fortified place: stronghold, *especially*: A large and permanent fortification sometimes including a town. A place that is protected against attack. This book seeks to describe what is a "Fortress Church". We would be looking into the dynamics of this Church as described in Jacob's vision in Genesis Chapter 28, also as described by the Prophet Isaiah, in Isaiah Chapter 2 and as the one detailed in a Psalm of the sons of Korah in Psalms Chapter 48. We would also be looking at a working model of this type of church as found at Antioch in the Book of Acts. Finally we would be exploring The Church at Ephesus, where the Apostle Paul by the Holy Spirit revealed some powerful descriptions of The Church.

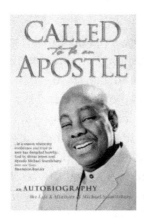

CALLED TO BE AN APOSTLE

This autobiography spans fifty-two years of my life on the earth thus far and I have the hope of living several more... Our home was always packed with young people and we did enjoy times of really wonderful fellowship! Although we were experiencing these wonderful times of fellowship my appetite and desire to grow in the things of God continued unabated. I continued to read anything and everything that I could put my hands on that would strengthen my life. I began reading Wigglesworth, Moody, Finney, Idahosa, Lake, and the list went on and on! But the more I read the more this question burned in my heart–"*why is it that every time we hear/read about a move of God, it is always miles away and in another country? Why can't I experience some of the things that I am reading about?*" Little did I know the Lord would answer that desire!

LEAVENED REVEALED

The Bible has a lot to say about *leaven* and its effects upon the Believer. Leaven as an ingredient gives a false sense of growth. In the New Testament there are at least six types of *leaven* spoken about and we will be exploring them in detail, in order to ensure that our lives are completely free of the first five, and completely influenced by the sixth! These types of leaven include the following: The leaven of the Pharisees; The leaven of the Sadducees; The leaven of the Galatians; The leaven of Herod; The leaven of the Corinthians. However, the Leaven of the Kingdom of God is the only type of leaven that has the power and capacity to bring about true growth and lasting change to our lives.

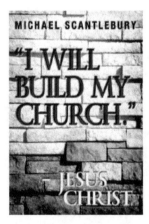

I WILL BUILD MY CHURCH
— JESUS CHRIST

"For we are his *masterpiece*, created in Christ Jesus for good works that God prepared long ago to be our way of life." Ephesians 2:10

What a powerful picture of The Church of Jesus Christ–His Masterpiece! Reference to a *masterpiece* lends to the idea that there are other pieces and among them all, this particular one stands head and shoulders above the rest! This is so true when it comes to The Church that Jesus Christ is building; when you place it alongside everything else that God has created, The Church is by far His Masterpiece!

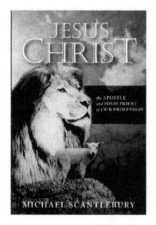

JESUS CHRIST THE APOSTLE AND HIGH PRIEST OF OUR PROFESSION

There is a dimension to the apostolic nature of Jesus Christ that I would like to capture in His one-on-one encounters with several people during the time He walked the face of the earth and functioned as Apostle. In this book we will explore several significant encounters that Jesus Christ had with different people where valuable principles and insight can be gleaned. They are designed to change your life.

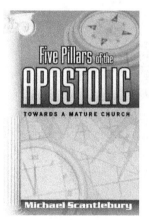

FIVE PILLARS OF THE APOSTOLIC

It has become very evident that a new day has dawned in the earth, as the Lord restores the foundational ministry of the Apostle back to His Church. This book will give you a clear and concise understanding of what the Holy Spirit is doing in The Church today.

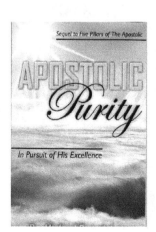

APOSTOLIC PURITY

In every dispensation, in every move of God's Holy Spirit to bring restoration and reformation to His Church, righteousness, holiness and purity has always been of utmost importance to the Lord. This book will challenge your to walk pure as you seek to fulfil God's Will for your life and ministry.

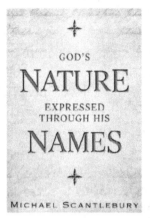

GOD'S NATURE EXPRESSED THROUGH HIS NAMES

How awesome it would be when we encounter God's Nature through the varied expressions of His Names. His Names give us reference and guidance as to how He works towards and in us as His people–and by extension to society! As a matter of fact it adds a whole new meaning to how you draw near to Him; and by this you can now begin to know His Ways because you have come into relationship with His Nature.

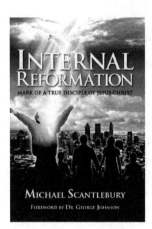

INTERNAL REFORMATION

Internal Reformation is multifaceted. It is an ecclesiology laying out the blue print of The Church Jesus Christ is building in today's world. At the same time it is a manual laying out the modus operandi of how Believers are called to function as dynamic, militant over-comers who are powerful because they carry internally the very character and DNA of Jesus Christ.

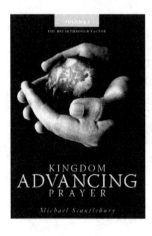

KINGDOM ADVANCING PRAYER VOLUME I

The Church of Jesus Christ is stronger and much more determined and equipped than she has ever been, and strong, aggressive, powerful, Spirit-Filled, Kingdom-centred prayers are being lifted in every nation in the earth. This kind of prayer is released from the heart of Father God into the hearts of His people, as we seek for His Glory to cover the earth as the waters cover the sea.

APOSTOLIC REFORMATION

If the axe is dull, And one does not sharpen the edge, Then he must use more strength; But wisdom brings success." (Ecclesiastes 10:10) For centuries The Church of Jesus Christ has been using quite a bit of strength while working with a dull axe (sword, Word of God, revelation), in trying to get the job done. This has been largely due to the fact that she has been functioning without Apostles, the ones who have been graced and anointed by the Lord, with the ability to sharpen.

KINGDOM ADVANCING PRAYER VOLUME II

Prayer is calling for the Bridegroom's return, and for the Bride to be made ready. Prayers are storming the heavens and binding the "strong men" declaring and decreeing God's Kingdom rule in every jurisdiction. This is what we call Kingdom Advancing Prayer. What a *Glorious Day* to be *Alive* and to be in the *Will* and *Plan of Father God*! *Hallelujah*!

KINGDOM ADVANCING PRAYER VOLUME III

One of the keys to the amazing rise to greater functionality of The Church is the clear understanding of what we call Kingdom Advancing Prayer. This kind of prayer reaches into the very core of the demonic stronghold and destroys demonic kings and princes and establishes the Kingdom and Purpose of the Lord. This is the kind of prayer that Jesus Christ engaged in, to bring to pass the will of His Father while He was upon planet earth.

IDENTIFYING AND DEFEATING THE JEZEBEL SPIRIT

I declare to you with the greatest of conviction that we are living in the days when Malachi 4:5-6 is being fulfilled. Elijah in his day had to confront and deal with a false spiritual order and government that was established and set up by an evil woman called Jezebel and her spineless husband called Ahab. This spirit is still active in the earth and in The Church; however the Lord is restoring His holy Apostles and Prophets to identify and destroy this spirit as recorded in Revelation 2:18-23.

CPSIA information can be obtained
at www.ICGtesting.com
Printed in the USA
LVHW081957210819
628472LV00018B/111/P